THE MAKING OF A JOURNALIST

Library of Journalism and Mass Media
A Continuing Series . . .

Part 1
ELEMENTS OF JOURNALISM, Mary J. J. Wrinn

Part 2
INTRODUCTION TO MODERN JOURNALISM, Stewart Robertson

Part 3
FREE-LANCE JOURNALISM AND SHORT STORY WRITING, Sydney A. Moseley

Part 4
THE PRINCIPLES OF JOURNALISM, Casper S. Yost

Part 5
HISTORY OF AMERICAN JOURNALISM, James M. Lee

Part 6
THE COMPLETE JOURNALIST. A STUDY OF THE PRINCIPLES AND PRACTICE OF NEWSPAPER-MAKING, F. J. Mansfield

Part 7
THE ART OF NEWSPAPER MAKING, Charles A. Dana

Part 8
THE MAKING OF A JOURNALIST, Julian Ralph

Part 9
PRINCIPLES OF NEWSPAPER MANAGEMENT, James E. Pollard

Part 10
THE INFLUENCE OF THE PRESS, R. A. Scott-James

THE MAKING OF A JOURNALIST

By

JULIAN RALPH

Author of "Our Great West"; "On Canada's Frontier"; "People We Pass"; "Alone in China"

COSMO PUBLICATIONS

2008 **New Delhi**

LIBRARY OF JOURNALISM AND MASS MEDIA
A CONTINUING SERIES
A SERIES OF CLASSIC READINGS

THE MAKING OF A JOURNALIST

First published by COSMO 2008

ISBN 81-307-0375-0 (Series)
ISBN 81-307-0383-1

Published by
COSMO PUBLICATIONS
for
GENESIS PUBLISHING PVT. LTD.
24-B, Ansari Road, Darya Ganj,
New Delhi-110 002,
INDIA

Printed in India by
Cosmo Publications

Contents

CHAP.		PAGE
I.	Choosing the Profession	1
II.	A "Nose for News"	14
III.	"Get What You're Sent For"	26
IV.	The Newspaper Interview	39
V.	Reporters of Crime	51
VI.	The Mysterious Sixth Sense	63
VII.	The War Correspondents	75
VIII.	The Dangers of War-Reporting	86
IX.	The Importance of Good-Nature	97
X.	A Wide Field of Action	113
XI.	The Power of a Reporter	124
XII.	The Value of Honesty	134
XIII.	Election Night	145
XIV.	The Special Correspondent	174

THE MAKING OF A JOURNALIST

I

CHOOSING THE PROFESSION

FOR a dozen years there has not been a month in which I have not been asked by friend and stranger to point out a course of study by which they can enter journalism. Boys and girls have been in the majority; but the interest in this outlet for talent and energy is by no means confined to them. Recently it was an officer in the British army who came to me for such advice. Still more recently it was an artist, who said that he needed the wonderful training of newspaper life, which forces men to disregard their inclinations and necessitates instant readiness for whatever work is demanded. While I stopped in London on my return from India the other day, a shrewd publisher assured me there was a great demand for such information in England; and, finally, in an American magazine, I read that there has not been attempted in America any effort worthy of the subject.

By drawing from twenty-five years of the most active experience in the newspaper business in America and Europe, varied by magazine work in the lines of travel and descriptive work—which is closer than a cousinship to newspaper work—I am going to tell what I know upon the subject. I will give the advice which I believe to be best for those who wish to enjoy and suffer the good and trying phases of this field of endeavor. It has its "grind," and that shall appear here. It has its dash and danger, its spice and glow, and these shall be described for all that they amount to. It has its honors and prizes; it carries with it importance to some who should stick to it and drudgery to others who should leave it — and this I will explain. And through all that follows the reader shall have incident, example, illustration, and story to clarify and illuminate the text.

Newspaper life, with its prizes and disappointments, is not a narrow field or a little subject—not if one realizes how wide one can stray without losing touch with it. Napoleon not only depended upon the press to prepare France for his plans and to execute many of them, but he directed and worked the newspapers in a way which was instinct with the spirit and genius of journalism. Bismarck's death leaves him revealed to us as an editorial manipulator of newspapers in a way and to a degree which assures us that the spirit of the newspaper man, as well as a correct view of the power and processes of the press, was his. Both of these great men showed that newspaper methods, when sublimated, reach far towards the realms of genius.

The Marquis of Salisbury was once a writer for the press—on editorial lines, to be sure—and yet these brought him into contact with the men and machinery of newspaperdom, and his ampler, mightier career cannot but have been affected by the experience. These examples reflect the spirit or genius of newspaper work; but how many know that there is even a monarch on one of the grandest thrones with whom the journalists half seriously claim a sort of mental kinship? His recent journey to the Holy Land was very like such a "sensation" as a modern millionaire-journalist might conceive and carry out to "increase circulation" — or popularity, in the case of an individual. The hasty ending of the trip, when it was found not to produce the stir that was expected, was also journalistic. Journalists see something of the same element in his mode of compelling popular interest in his navy, his addresses, and in his short, quick dashes into music and the other arts; but these are things of temperament mainly.

When we come to actual writers, some are literary, some are didactic, and some are journalistic, as Dickens was in all he wrote—and Boswell and Samuel Pepys, or, to go further back, as Seutonius and Plutarch were. The greatest feat of exploration — greatest because of its wholly human interest — was but a bit of reporting. I mean Stanley's finding of Livingstone. There are not many men who could carry off such a feat in the way it was done by Stanley, but do not for a moment think that there are not many who would not like to try it. There are thousands in America and in England who rise every morning hoping, praying, waiting for the orders to do work of that or any other dangerous, big, or difficult nature. Personal bravery is not scarce. Even love of risk and danger are literally a drug in the newspaper market to-day. I am going to tell of that in a chapter by itself.

At different times two powerful men of affairs, both gold-magnets who had attracted millions of dollars to their purses, and both large employers of men, commented upon my choice of a profession when I was interviewing them. Each did so from his own point of view of the moment. The one was what we call a "Lumber King." He had to do with a case at law which attracted the attention of all Christendom. It was the trial of Henry Ward Beecher, the noted anti-slavery agitator and popular preacher. Believing that this millionaire knew of something in which the public was keenly interested, I followed him for days—as I would have followed a balloon, a kidnapped girl, or the general in command of an army.

To illustrate why I did this, let me say that one day a friend of mine met a cowboy fifty miles from any town or camp, dragging a steer by a rope. He had lost his horse and was walking. The sun was tropical, water was nowhere to be had, Indians were likely to appear and kill him; still he tugged at his burden, which was harder to pull than if it had been dead. My friend inquired where he was dragging the "cow," and was told that the cowboy's destination was a place two days distant on horseback.

"Why!" my friend exclaimed, "what makes you try to pull a cow all that distance?"

"Because I've got it to do," was the laconic answer of the cowboy.

That is at once the motto, the excuse, and the exultant battle-cry of every earnest worker on the press: "I've got it to do." Until he has a thing to do it may not interest him at all; he may even congratulate himself that he is not called upon for the work in question. But when the order is given he is elated, nerved up, and pushed forward in a degree which swells with the difficulty of the task.

I pursued my millionaire because I had it to do. I sat on his doorstep until midnight. I was at his house before breakfast. I sent in my card wherever he called on business or his social rounds. At last, at one o'clock in the night, he bade me come in. "I am amazed at your persistence and patience and diligence," he said. "It is marvellous to me. I cannot understand why you do it, or how any employer finds men who will persevere as you have done—for mere wages. Of one thing I am sure: I am reputed to be worth millions, but if I could employ such men as work on the press I should be worth ten times what I am. Such self-sacrifice is not known in any other business."

But there was yet another view. I remembered what Commodore Vanderbilt, the founder of the Vanderbilt wealth and family, had said to me. He was leaning out of his light wagon behind the fastest pair of horses in America, for I had insisted upon interviewing him.

"You have mastered the intricacies of a very complex business matter," said he, "which has been the subject of thought and study with me for years. That you can do this and still remain in the newspaper business is very remarkable. Why do you do it? What do you gain by it? You are only just at the edge of manhood and are getting the wages of a clerk. Stay in the business and you may eventually make five times as much, but it will still be wages; you will still be working for others, and as you grow older you must work harder and harder. Take my earnest advice: leave newspapers alone and go into something that offers a better chance—something that will give you a solid reward—that will let you rest when you are tired."

By taking up this subject the shrewd old man avoided telling me the news for which I had come to him. What he said amounts to *Punch's* advice—"Don't." Believe me, it is good advice to most of those who will read this. Don't even try journalism unless you are certain it is your forte. In the United States — and in England, also, now that the press is undergoing a revolution there — it offers more money at the start than comes with almost any other line of work. It continues to return good pay to those who prove themselves its masters. But its training tends to prevent the formation of habits of thrift, to make men careless of the future; and it demands high-pressure service to the end, even when one's energies have to be worked up with a forced draught.

Do you aim at a large income for life? How many large salaries are paid in all newspaperdom? Compare the number of the lucky ones with the number who are poorly paid. Do you aim at editorial control of a newspaper? How many men have got such control as compared with the men who work for them — a dozen in fifteen hundred, say. And of that dozen how many control paying properties? Far fewer yet — fewer than you would believe unless you happen to be in the secrets of the calling.

No born man of the press will deny the other side of the case—namely, that if the microbe is in your blood, facts and figures may go hang themselves, and hardship, exposure, danger will only serve to push you further in. The prospect of a whole lifetime's incessant strain and toil will prove but as the sauce to the dish. You might as well ask the coming Nelson if he has thought what a dog's life a sailor's is. You might equally as well reason with the round-headed youth who itches to be a poorly paid human target in the front rank when England and Russia breathe hot in each other's faces in Asia.

How may any man or woman, boy or girl, know whether he or she is fitted to try this singular life? By any course of study? That is useless and impracticable except he be going into editorial work, and even then he should begin as a reporter and rise up to the other work. It is not good to enter a ship by the cabin window. You cannot direct sailors unless you know the ropes yourself. For every branch of journalism the education of a printing-office used to be all that was necessary, and the printing-offices turned out good material. To-day we think a sound common-school education is better and a college training is better yet. But education, or the lack of it, should not either rejoice or deter any earnest youth who is going to join the press, for service there is in itself an education, and to get its benefits the main requirement is to be naturally gifted or fitted for it.

How shall the candidate know whether he is qualified? First, I should say, by his study of his own inclination, and next by what he knows or is told by good judges of his ability as a letter-writer. Whoever cannot freely and easily write a good, readable, informing or amusing letter cannot write at all; whoever does, with ease and pleasure, write good letters *may* be able to write for the press. Good literature should be studied, and constant practice is a fine teacher. I once asked a man whose "style" is greatly admired by good judges, what book had influenced him most. "Boswell's *Johnson*, undoubtedly," he replied; "I am always picking it up and reading it." General Grant's *Memoirs* is an excellent model. Stevenson's *Treasure Island* is a magnificent specimen of clear, graphic, crisp, and yet rich composition. But read any of a hundred other writers whose work has stood in high rank for longer than a generation: the Bible first; then Shakespeare; after those, Thackeray, Scott, Emerson, Holmes, Balzac, and Victor Hugo. If money is lacking and books are hard to procure, be content with the Bible and *Robinson Crusoe*. You are not likely ever to learn to do better writing than is in those two books.

This point settled, the next thing is to write something for a newspaper. The press is not a charmed circle nor a secret fraternity. It is wide open and all-devouring. If I were stranded in a city or town and needed money I would walk the streets until I saw something novel or peculiar to the place, and that I should describe as I saw it, for the best newspaper there. I should not look for news. No one looks for that any more. That is an old-fashioned idea which outsiders will persist in retaining. News is now gathered systematically by men stationed at all the outlets of it, like guards at the gates of a walled city, by whom nothing can pass in or out unnoticed. You might start in chubby and beardless and grow bald and bent while looking for news without ever finding any.

Look for something human, pathetic, picturesque, humorous, or peculiar in some way or other—then write that. Make a "special article," as we say. Nothing is too old or hackneyed—the flight of a runaway cab, the torturing of a neighborhood by a talking parrot, the behavior and comments of the crowd at a fire—any one of ten millions of subjects will serve, provided you know how to bring out whatever it was that interested you. Two or three such bits of work will be more apt to get you a place on a paper than anything else that you can do.

One way that I have seen to work successfully is to go to a newspaper office and sit there every day, all day, for weeks; another is to report there every morning until it happens that something is wanted when no one else is by. But these methods require capital to live on and patience for a bedfellow. And at the end you still must prove your worth by writing. Then write to begin with. It is the simplest and best way to get on. Above all, do not easily be discouraged. I wrote occasionally for the magazines for thirteen years before I had an article accepted by one.

On the other hand, I became a newspaper writer in a day by describing the antics of a mad bull in the streets of a village. One of the very ablest men who has served in American journalism simply sent a naïve request to be taken on the New York *Sun* and enclosed his photograph. The method was so singular that it succeeded. A journalist who is now managing a London paper began by asking for a place as a reporter on a newspaper, and was told that there was no such place vacant, but that a man who could manage a typewriter was sorely needed. He took the typewriter's place, and, once inside the office, worked his way speedily upon the staff by such "special" writing as I have described. Mr. Kennedy Jones, one of the brightest of the new-school journalists of London, wrote a series of articles describing the typical characters of Glasgow in order to get a place on a newspaper in that city. To-day he described the life of a city clerk, next week he took up the shop-girl, after that the car-driver, and did the work in such a manner as to be eagerly taken on. One of the greatest book reviewers in America, who then had no experience, but needed employment, walked into a newspaper office and asked for work. The editor took a book off his desk and said, "Review that." He wrote such a scholarly article—and so promptly—that he earned a hundred dollars a week at once and double as much soon afterwards. Horace Greeley, Mark Twain, and scores of others began as printers' "devils"—a route into journalism which is still certain to be followed for a long time to come—in country journalism in America, at all events.

One day a college professor applied to an editor for a place, and the editor said to me: "This man is from my college and I want to oblige him. Please think out something that he can do which requires no training." I suggested that he read the foreign papers and pick out of them the uncommon and the human things and notes of queer customs which have endured since ancient days. He came and succeeded at once. I mention this because it is such a singular case. As a rule, when a man applies for a position, he is the one who must do the necessary thinking.

II

A "Nose for News"

ALL our senses are mysterious, but there is one which journalists—and only a few others—have, in addition to the rest, that is even more strange. I do not refer to their weird "sixth sense," which leads them to the discovery of news, sometimes against their inclination and even against their judgment, as a hypnotist bends his subject to his will. I shall speak of that later.

First of all, every journalist ranks what is called his newspaper sense, or "sense of news." If you are a candidate or a beginner you cannot tell whether you have this gift or not until you have repeatedly tried yourself. It is simply the light or intuition by which you know what to write and what to leave out, what to make the most of, what is worth a paragraph, and what is worth a whole page of a newspaper. I will illustrate this with a story. It is necessary to begin it by explaining that Frederic Hudson, once a great manager of the New York *Herald*, held to a theory that a newspaper should have some one great piece of news or story of wide interest in every issue.

Of course, it is impossible to have a great battle fought or a pope elected or a city fall by an earthquake every evening in time for us all to read about it at breakfast next morning. And yet Frederic Hudson's idea was practicable, and he knew it—because he possessed the faculty called the "news sense." He had "a nose for news," as some men express it. He could scent news out as some persons believe that a divining-rod feels the presence of precious metals in the ground, or as another sort of sprig or rod is affected when it is taken over any place where the earth hides a spring or course of water. The late Senator Hearst must have had some such implement in his make-up, for every old California miner will tell you that he was able to feel or see or smell the presence of gold in the rocks as he roamed over the foot-hills of the Rocky Mountains, locating rich mine after rich mine.

Ballard Smith, the distinguished managing editor and London correspondent, believed with Hudson, and also had the news sense highly developed. One afternoon, in what is called the "silly season" in London newspaper circles, there was not a speck of news stirring beyond the routine list of fourth-rate happenings. Mr. Smith sent for me and asked me to help him read the afternoon papers and try to "make a piece of news" for the next day's issue. I knew his method, and we both read every paragraph of news matter, and even such advertisements as we suspected might hide a tiny nugget which we could beat out into what he desired.

"I have it!" he cried out after half an hour's reading, and, catching up a pair of shears, he clipped out a three-line paragraph and handed it to me. It was simply an announcement that a tiny baby girl had been found in a vacant plot of ground in Harlem. The only uncommon feature of the case was that the infant was richly dressed.

"There!" said he, triumphantly. "It is five o'clock, and by midnight we should have a page, or nearly a page, of this in type or ready to be set up. You write the main story. See the place where the baby was found, the policeman who found it; follow it to Matron Webb's room in the police headquarters, where all foundlings are first taken, and get a long, full account from the matron of her experience with such cases—the most remarkable, strangest, most pathetic, moving, or stirring experiences she has had. Then jump into a cab and go to the asylum where these babies are brought up, and to the Potter's Field where they are buried. The idea is to hang the whole story of the treatment of foundlings upon the case of this beautiful, richly dressed baby which you are to use as the text. Before you start, map out work bearing on the subject for the rest of the staff to do. You can have twenty reporters if you need them. We will drop everything else and tell the public, for the first time, the story of a foundling."

I forget how many reporters were put upon this task, but the majority worked with that enthusiasm which alone could produce the desired result, and we published a long and absorbingly interesting story next day. We made known the unlooked-for tenderness and care which foundlings met with while in the hands of the rough policeman and the kindly woman who first takes charge of them. Very different was their after-fate, ending with the speedy burial of the startlingly great majority in trenches, several in each trench, with only numbers to distinguish them. This was legitimate, dignified, and true journalism—the only sort that was practised upon that newspaper. Of no other sort of press methods do I intend to speak in these chapters, except it be to point a moral or otherwise to exhibit them in the light from which their votaries shrink.

One day I reported to my "chief," Charles A. Dana, the fact that a man had called to show us some leather which he had made of a human skin. "Ugh!" exclaimed the chief. "Show him out of the door." I then said that news had come of the arrest of a distinguished New Hampshire man for theft. "Go yourself," said the chief; "send us all you can get about it." His news sense worked instantly and accurately.

What will the public enjoy reading? What will prove interesting to the greater number of the people? To be able to answer these questions correctly, instinctively, a score of times a day and every day in the year—that is what it is to have the news sense. It is not exclusively the newspaper man's gift, for novelists, playwrights, and theatre-managers, among others, are dependent upon something very like it for success. This gift has made a unique place for one man who is actually able to play with his faculty and caricature its processes. I refer to Mr. R. F. Hamilton, who devises the advertising for a great American show now established in England. His alleged discovery that oysters can be educated, and his announcement of an indignation meeting of the human curiosities to protest against being called "freaks," are examples of how this gift can be so ingeniously exaggerated that even the greatest newspaper may not suspect either the method or the purpose.

This news sense and the spirit of enterprise are so often bound together in modern journalism that it is not easy to say where one leaves off or the other begins. Both were equal in the newspaper proprietors who despatched Stanley to find Livingstone, and the same was the case when only one editor among the thousands who read of the kidnapping of a white maiden by Canadian Indians had the impulse to send a reporter instantly to visit the savages and discover the fate of the girl.

It was the mastering power of both the news sense and enterprise combined which sent Mr. Bonsal to the capital of Morocco with his life in his hand, and later to be the first passenger locked up, helplessly, in a submarine boat. "What goes up must come down," says a homely proverb, but in the case of this boat it was by no means so certain that what went down must come up.

In my own experience, the combination of impulses once operated in a way which makes me smile when I recall it. I went with Mr. Remington, the artist, all the way to the Rocky Mountains to see the "sun dance" of the Blackfeet Indians, but when we reached the Indian grounds we found that we were five weeks early.

At that point the news sense had done all it could. Then enterprise rose up in us, and we hired the chief and his head men to order the whole tribe or nation to do their great religious dance for us in advance of the regular season. It cost a chest of tea, plenty of sugar, still more money, and a large quantity of tobacco, but the whole tribe performed for us with such mad enthusiasm that we were not quite certain we should not figure at the end as human sacrifices to their deities.

We had let loose all the savagery there was in that great reach of wild nature. But we found that there were limits even to the power of money, for on no account would the old chief permit us to take his photograph once he discovered that the camera employed the mysterious and (to him) awful forces of the sun to do its work. On the other hand, money would have bought for us the last thing we should have thought it could purchase — human suffering.

The young bucks of the tribe who, having made a successful hunting journey, are ready to be enrolled as warriors, undergo revolting self-torture in the "sun dance" in order to impress the others with their bravery and hardiness. This shocking sight was mercifully omitted from the dance as it was performed for us, but when we made inquiries as to the degree of pain and the length of torture it involved, the chief kindly offered to order any number of his young men that we desired to perform the operation for our enlightenment—at five dollars each!

The most laughable and the most extraordinary experience I ever had in newspaper work brings out with a bold stroke the force which the news sense has when it exerts itself upon its subjects. It was in the days when the "Molly Maguires" were at last being brought to deserved grief. These Molly Maguires to which I refer were not the original lawless Irish band of that name, but a secret fraternity of coal-miners who herded together to terrorize the people in the Pennsylvania coal region with murder, arson, and violence of every nature. Two or more were about to be hanged at one of the mining centres, and many reporters assembled there. Among them was an unpopular one who was very credulous. He came to the rest of us for the news which he should have obtained for himself. From what I sorrowfully confess was a misguided sense of humor, I made him believe that the people dreaded an attack upon the town and an attempt to rescue the condemned men from the jail. He sent my rigmarole to his paper, and though the rest of us laughed in our sleeves, it turned out that he thus put a plume in his cap and made himself appear more clever than we.

On that night we went to bed, only to be startled out of our sleep by what appeared to be a fusillade of rifle-shots. I had heard the same sound before, and knew it to be that of torpedoes affixed to the tracks of the neighboring railway by the men of one coal train to warn the crew of the next train that their way ahead was not clear. Therefore, I meant to turn over and go to sleep again. But it was not to be. Some of my reporter friends burst into my room and bade me dress with all haste. The Molly Maguires were attacking the town, they said.

"But that is all nonsense," I answered; "it is the romance I invented this afternoon."

And so it was. But I and every other reporter there were obliged, none the less, to flash the alleged news to all the New York papers, for the following strange reason: The silly fellow at whose expense I had amused myself had gone all over the place repeating my story and insisting that he had it upon the best authority. He had so excited the people that the leading ones had formed themselves into a special police force, had armed themselves, and were patrolling the streets and waiting and listening with nerves strained to the breaking-point. Others had discovered a band of mysterious but very substantial men camped around a fire in the woods just outside the town, and these were believed to be but biding their time for making the attack. No one had been to bed except the reporters. Thus a mere practical joke set to work forces which developed news that could not be disregarded, and I was obliged to telegraph the tale with which I had, a few hours earlier, amused myself.

But the Frenchman who said "it is the unexpected which happens" expressed in a phrase the character of all news and the constant experience of the reporter. Two days after my own invention turned to reality, I followed the bodies of the executed outlaws to the village where they had misspent their lives. I was bent upon describing the "wake" which I knew would precede their burial. Nothing seemed more certain or simple than the execution of this plan, yet I did not carry it out.

What a strange phase of existence I see as I think back on that little coal-mining village—what an anachronism it was to exist in this century—how misplaced in our free and enlightened land! Death was not only in the cabins of the two cowardly assassins; its swart shadow hung like a pall over the entire place. The only man who walked boldly in the single street was the mine boss or foreman, and he was girt about with pistols and guarded by stalwart constables of the Coal and Iron Police, who followed him like two shadows, armed with carbines. The "Mollies" had sworn to take his life as they had taken scores of others, yet he stayed there and went on with his work. He strode the street boldly, but the other men slunk in and out and to and fro like cats—or panthers.

I went into a cabin of the dead, and the crooning ceased, the very air grew chilly, every man turned his back upon me; the women alone faced me, but with hatred in their looks. No one offered me a welcome, a chair, or a share of the feasting. The press had stirred the authorities to break up their band; had I been the law personified I could not have been more unwelcome. I sat down, but not for long. A ruffian lurched over to me and asked if I was a reporter.

"Yes; what then?"

"Well, you're not wanted here," said he.

I saw that he meant more than that. Bidding them all good-bye, I strode out with my face composed to express the utmost sang-froid. I looked about the tiny village, hating to give up my task, wondering what to do. As I lounged in front of a shop-window I became aware that the shopkeeper was beckoning me in.

"Are you the New York reporter?"

"Yes."

"Then take my advice and leave this village at once. The men have sworn to kill you if you stay after sundown."

I took the advice because I could get nothing by staying. So, at sunset, I left the village and climbed the bare face of the mountain beside it—as conspicuous a target and as complete an advertisement of defeat as ever was mortal man.

III

"Get What You're Sent For"

THE life of every journalist is as hard as nails; that of the special correspondent is even harder—yet neither one knows it, nor asks for sympathy. When we appreciate this fact we begin to understand the familiar adage, "The Lord tempers the wind to the shorn lamb."

These men see their strained, exciting, never-halting toil through glasses colored by sentiment or through the heat-waves of excitement. They are forever stimulated by competition and freshened by constant novelty. They wonder that their friends pity them; yet it is a fact that they can make no engagements ahead; their time, their leisure, their very lives are not their own. The year around, others stop work at sunset, but when the newspaper writer works his day is from noon until sunrise. Though it has grown to be an iron service, many of us know how differently it began.

It was once a haphazard, unmethodical business, managed by printers and led by geniuses, ne'er-do-wells, Bohemians—often men of disorderly lives or irresponsible natures, who lived very much as the performers on the stage continued to do long after journalism became a systematized science. To-day there are geniuses on the press, but they are calm and self-controlled. What are termed "Bohemians" still follow the calling, but they wear clean linen, live comfortably, and are only called "Bohemians" because they do not take life as seriously as most persons. In these days all newspaper men must be ready for work at every moment of every day; they must be sober; they must appear well, and they must be able at least to present the external signs of refinement.

I have to look back only twenty years to remember when neither the pay nor the demands upon a journalist in New York warranted his having a suit of evening clothes. Very funny situations resulted from this. I recollect when one of the best reporters in America was made wretched by being ordered to report the Charity Ball, then the greatest and smartest social event of the year in that city. He was obliged to see the people and the dresses and the dancing, and yet he knew he would not be allowed on the dancing-floor in ordinary attire. The plan he hit upon for overcoming this difficulty was peculiar. He bought a white tie, an opera-hat, and a pair of white gloves, and instead of going to the coat-room, he wandered about the lobbies with his coat buttoned, his hat under one arm, and his tie and gloves showing conspicuously so as to suggest that he was properly clad under his great-coat. A year afterwards he went upon another newspaper, and when I asked him how he liked his new employers he said: "It is a perfect establishment. They always keep a man with a dress-suit on the staff."

Captain Ronald F. Coffin, the author of many notable sea tales, used to tell with gusto how he was sent at about this time to a great house to report a meeting of the Nineteenth Century Club. He was a well-to-do man, with at least three houses of his own and money in bank, but he was obliged to stand or fall with the others in the business who were not all such substantial citizens as he. On this occasion the lady of the house saw him seated in the drawing-room, which opened upon a dining-room that had been arranged for a large dinner-party and was lustrous with plate and crystal. She called up to her husband to know who was "the person" in the drawing-room, and the captain heard his host reply that he was a reporter. Upon learning this, the lady crept into the dining-room and, gathering up all the silver spoons and forks, made off with them out of his reach. I am sure that if the cautious lady knew how he laughed at this feat of hers she would smile at it herself.

Captain Coffin's history illustrates another of the manifold routes which men pursue in order to enter the guild of journalism. It also serves to show how various are the sorts of men who drift into the business. He had been the popular captain of a fast packet-ship sailing between Liverpool and New York, and when the civil war broke out he enlisted in the navy and commanded a blockading vessel, on which he distinguished himself by his courage. When the war ended, he went, one Sunday morning, to hear the Rev. Henry Ward Beecher preach. There, for the first time, he saw short-hand reporters taking down each word as it fell from the lips of the gifted orator. It struck him that this was a calling he might learn and live by, and so, at past the middle age, he conquered the rather simple science. With this equipment he secured a place on a newspaper, but his sea knowledge was of more value than stenography, and he became the chief yachting and marine writer of the American newspapers.

One day, Mr. Oakey Hall, an ex-mayor of New York and also a journalist, sent him to report a fashionable wedding in Grace Church. It was like sending a scientist to criticise Madame Bernhardt's acting, or like asking a musical critic to describe a panic on the Stock Exchange. The old captain went to the church, but was met at the door by Sexton Brown, a famous character at the time. "No reporters will be allowed in the church," said the sexton, sternly. "You don't know how glad I am," the captain replied; "I was dreadfully afraid you were going to let me in." While he was absent from his office a cartoonist, who had heard of the strange errand upon which he had been sent, drew a cartoon showing the old man in sailor dress interviewing the sexton and asking "How was the bride rigged?"

Those days are gone. To-day a well-equipped journalist must be able to manage any sort of reporting and to appear in every sort of company. Many such writers have had more or less intimate acquaintance with the leaders of mankind—the Bismarcks and Gladstones, the Gordons and Grants, the Deweys and Beresfords. Journalism has put me on the pleasantest footing with more than one President of the United States. The first President I came to know was General Arthur. Four or five of us correspondents were sent to the St. Lawrence to report his experiences upon a fishing-trip. We lived in the same hotel with him, and in the mornings he used to share with us the muskalonge or the bass he had caught on the previous day. And once it came about that he waited upon me as if he had been the humblest man in the land.

With another correspondent I had been kept up late at night telegraphing, and then had stayed up still later over a midnight supper. When we came to the hotel it was past midnight and the entire house—except the windows of the President's suite of seven rooms—was dark and lifeless. His windows were still brilliantly lighted, for it was his habit to work or read until very late at night. We tried all the doors, and when we came to the last one, President Arthur opened it and let us in. We apologized profusely, but he only smiled and said that as his negro boy was very tired and had gone to sleep, he thought he would rather let us in himself than disturb his servant.

"You have found very agreeable society here," he said.

"No," we replied; "we have been telegraphing."

"Don't tell me that," he insisted; "you telegraph only about me, and I have done nothing for twenty-four hours. I prefer to envy you, and to believe that you have found some one's society very charming."

To give an idea of the rigid discipline of a modern newspaper establishment, I will recall the trivial fact that when I was new and green upon the staff of such a paper I once missed a train which I had been ordered to take. "Impossible!" exclaimed the editor when I reported the fact. "Let me tell you, sir, that reporters upon this paper never miss trains." A month passed before I could feel that this offence was forgotten, and during that month how many feats of persistency and enterprise I performed in order to get back a good opinion of myself! Most of these performances were never heard of by my superiors.

I remember that I was very much elated over being trusted with such an important task as reporting the execution of a negro murderer at Hempstead, Long Island. I will not dilate upon the horror of seeing such a sight for the first time, or tell how that feeling was increased by the fact that the murderer and I recognized each other as old acquaintances—for he had been a vagabond who idled about the neighborhood where I had lived as a child. He even made a comical face at me as he passed me on his way to the scaffold. When the last scene had been enacted and I was leaving the jail in a leisurely way, I spied another reporter, upon a rival paper, running at full speed across the plain to get to the telegraph-office ahead of me. He was an old hand and I was a boy. He worked for rich employers and could pay to keep the telegraph busy for hours, so that I would not be able to send in a word of my report.

I had no other advantage except what came of being younger than he. I ran after him with all my might, and presently, when we were neck and neck, the plain became a sheet of ice, glaring, smooth as window-glass, difficult to pass over even at the slowest gait. Still we forged ahead. Presently we came to a depression—a gully—and he kept on the level ground while I ran into the cutting. He was beating me; my strength and wind were giving out. Just when I thought I must allow myself to be beaten and disgraced, I saw him slip and slide, and in another second he had fallen down the tall side of the gully to lie stunned and torn and bleeding at my feet.

"I am hurt," he cried; "will you help me to the village?"

"Will you give me the first chance at the telegraph?" I asked.

"Yes, I am beaten; I acknowledge it," he answered.

So I helped him to the town and looked after him—but took care to send my report in ahead of his.

The same spirit engendered by the strict discipline of modern journalism actuated Thomas B. Fielders, of the *Times*, in New York, and later of the *Pall Mall Gazette*, of London. He had boarded an ocean steamship at the Quarantine Station in New York Harbor, and had obtained the news for which he had been sent, but when he tried to return to his office he was told that he could not leave the ship until the next morning. What do you suppose he did? Seeing a sailing-vessel sliding along far below, but close to the towering side of the ship on which he was a prisoner, he leaped over the rail and down upon the deck of the moving vessel. Thus he alone of all the reporters on that errand was enabled to reach the city with his news. "Follow your copy if it blows out of the window," is the order printers always give to their apprentices. "Get what you're sent for, if you have to go through fire and water," is the corresponding injunction of the old hands to the new ones in journalism.

Another story which illustrates this same spirit is told of me. As I remember it, the tale is that, being ordered to accompany a train that was to attempt to beat the world's record for speed, I was thwarted by the railway managers, who proposed to give the privilege to the correspondent of a rival newspaper. Then, according to the story,

I at once set out for a city on the route where I knew that all trains are required to run slowly within the town limits, and where I suspected a change of locomotives would be made. There I pleaded with the mayor to board the train and take me with him as his secretary. He did so, and I was able to report my sensations during the bullet-like journey.

We will not analyze this story. Its moral is unassailable. If a reporter gets what he is told to, he is a good reporter; if not, he is no good. There is no half-way in that course of schooling.

In England, one day, I sent a well-known journalist to a great party at a ducal house in order that he might describe for an American newspaper what went on there. He telegraphed me that he had been refused admission, and I naturally expected him to come back to London. On the contrary, that night I received by wire a splendid and intimate account of the festivities in question. When he returned I asked him how he got his facts. "I arranged with the bandmaster," said he, "that I should carry the music in and sort it out for the musicians. I carried it in, dressed in the uniform of the orchestra. I could not arrange the music, but when I was inside I sat down behind the bass-drum and saw all that I wanted to, without being noticed myself."

Some desperate and many inexcusable things are done in the name of newspaper enterprise, but others as well as myself can tell all who practise such methods that they only succeed for the moment, and that peril to both reporter and newspaper walks hand-in-hand with all fraud. There is a well-known literary man in London who, when he was a youth, ran off with a mail-bag which he knew contained a document that he wanted immediately, but which would not be delivered in due course until the next morning. He was chased and shot at by the mail agents, but managed to escape both injury and capture. Not a particle more defensible than this was the trick of the reporter who appeared in Rudyard Kipling's room dressed as a mechanic, and talked with the novelist in that guise. Here, however, is an instance of successful reporting over which many men may take sides and argue warmly for and against what the reporter thought fit to do.

When Li Hung Chang was in London, an American correspondent thought he would try to interview him, though he had heard that the queer old statesman would not talk to a reporter for publication under any circumstances. He called and said he was from America, and was instantly shown into the old man's presence. He got a long interview and bowed himself out. Afterwards he heard that Mr. Li supposed he was a member of a committee from America who had been sent to arrange his tour in that country. The strictest moralists will say that he should not have published a word of the interview, under the circumstances. I agree with them, but there are others who will argue differently.

To attain difficult ends, correspondents have had themselves shut up in prisons and in madhouses, have crossed the ocean in the steerage, have braved the terrors of the cholera in Hamburg and the plague in India, and have invaded every lawless land there is. With them, and with all others, the deeds they have done and the methods they have employed have been invariably weighed by their own consciences, and so it must ever be in such cases. The great statesman Gladstone, on one occasion, took the question out of the sphere of the correspondent's conscience and settled it himself. It was when Homer Davenport, the cartoonist from America, went to Hawarden to see the aged chieftain in order to familiarize himself with his face and draw it. He met Mr. Gladstone on the road near his house. He told him he was a tourist from Oregon.

"And did you come all the way from Oregon to see me?" Gladstone inquired.

"I did, sir," was Davenport's reply.

"Then," said the ex-premier, "all I can say is that you must be fond of travel. Good-morning, sir."

IV

The Newspaper Interview

A GREAT deal of nonsense and a great deal more of falsehood has been written about the once American habit of interviewing. I say the "once American" habit, because, while it grew to its present proportions as an institution in America, it is now the resort and delight of journalists all over Christendom. This had to be. In no other way can either public or private demands be satisfied where authoritative news and views are in demand than by the interview—except in the case of the London *Times*, which has gained, for its occasional utterances upon public affairs, the reputation of their being "inspired."

If M. Zola spends three months in England, we do not want to hear from a reporter what he thinks of the country. He alone can tell us, and if it does not occur to him to do so of his own accord, we must send and interview him. A journalist's account of what a great man thinks and feels is only slightly more valuable than a promising novel broken off by a great novelist's death and finished by a friend or some hack hired by a publisher. The feature of interviewing which most laymen fail to understand is that, seven in ten times, the man who is interviewed is glad of a chance to speak. The few who did not wish it when they were asked have said so much against the practice as to make most of us overlook the fact that one hundred or one thousand were interviewed, and wanted to be interviewed, for every one who declined.

When a man is full of a subject, or in dire trouble, or has set the world agog by some uncommon feat, he needs an outlet and welcomes the interviewer. The interviewer is to such a man what a safety-valve is to an idle boiler under pressure. An occurrence in the family of a late Lord High Chancellor of England once aroused the interest of the English-speaking world, and a correspondent attempted to interview another man who was concerned in the affair. "Why talk to me? Why not ask the Lord High Chancellor?" this person asked. "I will," replied the correspondent, and left the other man grinning at what he deemed the preposterous idea he had suggested. Nevertheless, the Lord High Chancellor granted his visitor a two-column interview. He had been anxious to free his mind, and the visit of the correspondent occurred just as he was most in the mood.

Crowfoot, the last great redskin chief of Canada, the head of the Canadian branch of the powerful Blackfeet tribe, was once interviewed in my presence by a deputation of ladies. He was a splendid man, kingly in every respect. He looked like the portraits of Julius Cæsar. He had commanded his nation in the days when the red Indians were the undisputed rulers of the best and biggest part of a continent, and had fought against incessant, ever-increasing odds, until at last his vassals had been pauperized by the government of the whites, careless, if not ignorant, of the valuable uses to which these finest savages the world has known could easily have been put. But to the last he was never less a king in spirit and bearing than when his tribe was exterminating its only rivals.

When the white women came to interview him he was seated in a railway sleeping-car, upon a spotless white blanket stretched over a bed. He wore eagle plumes in his long, jet hair. His coat was a huge bit of jewelry, being entirely covered with beads — snow-white, with a blazing sun worked upon its back and an elaborate design in colors upon its front. His two half-trousers were also of white beads, as rich as ivory or silver, patterned in blue and red. His moccasins were such that a collector would give fifty dollars for them to-day. It was all I could do to lift this royal suit of clothing when I saw it afterwards lying upon the ground in his tepee.

As the three white women advanced towards him, he threw from his face the sober expression which he usually wore, and smiled his welcome to them. I have always said, since I knew the red-man in the waning splendor of his glory, that no more perfect gentleman has ever been created, and this little anecdote will help to prove my words.

"Are you married, Crowfoot?" one woman inquired.

"No."

"What? Not married? Did you never have a wife?"

"No; not any wife."

"Oh, do tell us why! Is it possible so brave a man does not like women?"

Crowfoot had always been a woman-hater, but far from saying so rude a thing, he replied, after a moment's thought:

"Never any woman have me."

Some days later I interviewed both Crowfoot and a zealous old Catholic missionary and scholar, Père Lacombe, who, besides spending his long life with these romantic people, had written an authoritative dictionary of the parent tongue of the Western Canadian Indians. The priest and the chief conversed in the Creek tongue, and what became my surprise to see them warming up, in time, and laughing and nudging each other like two schoolmates who meet after a long separation and rehearse the adventures or the mischievous pranks in which they have taken part. This proved to be what they were really doing!

"What is it, father?" I asked.

Then the noble old priest told me that he and his warrior friend were recalling the days when the priest was missionary to both the Crow nation and the Blackfeet—tribes at such enmity to each other that the world was not large enough to hold them both. They recollected how one night, when the priest was ministering to the Blackfeet, an attack on the camp was made by the Crows. It was pitch dark, and along with the first notice came the rush of the enemy, the firing of their guns, the screaming of the Blackfeet squaws, the clamor of the startled dogs, and all the hubbub of primitive warfare. The priest thought to restore peace by his presence, and so he rushed into the mêlée, crying, "Stop this wickedness! Go to your wigwams, you Crows; do you hear me? I am your priest." He might as well have scolded a hurricane or tried to command a volcanic eruption. Bullets whistled by his ears, and warriors rushed headlong upon him. Then his manner changed. He saw that it was to be a fight to the death and that the only part of wisdom was to counsel strong self-defence.

"Here," he cried to the Blackfeet, "give me a gun. Rouse yourselves. Save your women and children and your own lives. Quick, I say; give me a gun and let us drive these mad people back to where they came from."

After that, side by side with Crowfoot, the priest fought; and the sight so stirred the braves behind him that the battle was easily won. And so was a still greater battle, because from that time the gentle scholar who came among them to preach love and mercy and faith in the true God had gained a hold upon the hearts of those rude warriors such as no other priest upon the continent has perhaps ever possessed.

Does any one suppose that there was ever a day in their lives after that thrilling event when both these men would not have liked to tell the story—if it came naturally and apropos of something, without being pulled out by the ears for mere self-glorification? So it is most of the time when an interviewer seeks what the crabbed and ill-natured people love to call "his prey."

I was once sent to interview a French Rothschild, a nobleman, but a youth of slight experience in the world. I was ordered to draw him out upon the subject of finance. I never took part in a stranger interview. He received me cordially because he thought I came from a great London paper of the same name as the American paper upon which I was employed. When I explained this he began to look blank.

"And for what haf I ze plaisure of zis veeseet?" he asked.

"I wish to speak to you of finance."

"Fynance?" he repeated, obviously puzzled by a word he had never heard.

"Yes," I repeated; "about finance."

His secretary now enlightened him.

"Oh, feenarnce! Oui, je comprends. Well, what will you tell me of feenarnce?"

"Nothing. I wish you to tell me something about it."

"I?" he repeated, in surprise. "My dear sir, I assure you I know nussing whatever about ze feenarnce."

"Neither do I," I replied, and, thanking him cordially, I left him, puzzled to this day, I do not doubt, to grasp the purpose of my visit. It was an ill-advised errand. There were a score of subjects in which he was interested and on which he could have been drawn out, but my editor, mistaking him for an aged banker, instead of a pleasure-loving youth, had chosen the wrong one.

The subject of an interview must be wisely chosen. It must interest the person called upon, must touch a responsive chord, or else it begins with unwarranted intrusion and ends with failure. After a topic has been well chosen or has forced itself upon the editor as the obvious one for a discussion of which the public is waiting, there is one other essential to success, and that is absolute accuracy in reporting the conversation. It often happens that one cannot take notes, or does not wish to do so. Note-books and pencils frequently alarm and put upon his guard a man who would talk freely in an ordinary conversation.

In all my experience, though I have even been obliged to challenge the accuracy of a Secretary of State, I have only once been forced to publish a correction of what I have written—and then I was right, and the correction was the falsehood. It was a singular case. I interviewed a vestryman of the richest church society in America, and he readily and vigorously expressed his opinion upon the subject in hand. On the next day, when he saw his words in print, he denied that he said that which I credited to him. More remarkable still, he came to the office where I was employed and said he had not been interviewed at all. He was told that my word would be regarded as equal to his, but that I would call upon him and he and I should decide upon what was to be done. When I called upon him he did not deny the truth of my report, but declared that he had been too impulsive, and his words had placed him in a very disagreeable position. He begged me as a personal favor to declare my report incorrect. I told him I would repeat his request to my editor, but I also took occasion to picture to him the serious plight in which such duplicity as his would have placed a younger journalist, who might yet have a reputation to make. In saying that my reports have never been found wanting in accuracy I do not boast. That is not a thing to boast of. It is the first necessity of a journalist to be accurate, and any man or newspaper that fails in this respect cannot prosper for long.

I remember another singular case when a slender young gentleman was sent to interview an architect whose bad work had led to the collapse of a semi-public building in New York. The architect listened to the young reporter's request for an interview, and then replied that if he did not leave his presence at once he would throw him out of the window. Thirty minutes later the architect once again heard a rap at his door and called out "Come in." In strode the biggest reporter in New York, who was also one of the largest men in the country. He weighed three hundred pounds, and it was of him that an Irishman, looking down from the gallery at the reporters at a public meeting, called out, "Oh, will yez luk at the soize of the man that is airnin' his livin' wid a little pincil!"

"What do you wish?" the architect inquired.

"I am another reporter," said the gigantic scribe, "sent to ask you to throw me out of the window instead of the man we sent here half an hour ago. He was too small to be worth your while, but I am different. And now, sir, you will either throw me out of the window or I will throw you out—or you will, more wisely, sit down and explain how you came to do such bungling work on that building."

The architect decided to grant the interview.

One day a President of the United States sent for me. He had been elected to that high office, but had not yet been installed.

"I hear," he said, "that you have just come back from Washington."

"Yes."

"Did you go to the White House? You did? Well, please sit down and tell me all about it. What sort of a house is it? How is it managed?

How many rooms are in it? Whereabouts does the President do his work? And how did you get in there—how do visitors manage to see the house while a President and his family are living in it?"

"Why," I exclaimed, "you have often been to Washington! Have you never visited the White House?"

"No," said he; "I have only seen the outside of it. I have never even seen a President, or, in fact, any great man. I am so peculiarly constituted that, if I knew the greatest man in the world could be seen by walking to the corner, I would not walk there. But now that I am about to make the White House my home, I should very much like to hear all that you can tell me about it."

Finally, there remains to be added to this slight treatise on interviewing an account of the funniest interview I ever had or heard of. My newspaper was the New York *Sun*, and it had sent me to look up some one in a suburb of the city. The address was a number in Fourth Street, but to my amazement I found three such streets in the place. The house I sought was not in any of them. Tired and almost discouraged, I turned into a cobbler's shop, and, seeing a bearded German bending over a last in the glare of a swinging lamp, I cleared my throat and said:

"I beg your pardon, but I am a reporter of the *Sun*—"

"Well, well," he said, soothingly, before I could finish the sentence, "you cannot help dot."

I could not continue for a full minute, so struck was I by the unexpected philosophy and wisdom of his reply. I could not help being a reporter, and I knew it. I had always believed I was born to be one, but who would have supposed a cobbler could have discovered all that by merely glancing at me?

A lovely old chap was this cobbler. I wish I could have run across him often, and learned to know him. When I explained that I wanted an address in Fourth Street, and had already been to three Fourth Streets, and would like to know if there were any more, he lifted his hammer and poised it in the air for half a minute.

"You vant to know if dere is some more of dose Fourt' Streets?" he asked. "Vell, I vill tell you. I haf lived here dwenty years, drying to find somedings owt, und I ditn't find anydings owt yet."

V

Reporters of Crime

THERE has grown up with the development of the modern newspaper a class of correspondents who are chosen to ferret out the perpetrators of mysterious crimes, and to secure news whose possessors are doing their utmost to conceal it from the public.

Some call themselves "detective reporters," but this implies the possession of some mysterious gift, whereas the work requires nothing but a liking for it, a clearness of brain, and an indomitable perseverance. Without these no reporter or correspondent can ever become great in his profession. The only men on the press who can thrive without these qualities are the editorial and the descriptive writers. For my part, I do not believe that professional detectives require any higher qualities. We were all very highly entertained by Dr. Conan Doyle's conception of the wizard-like Sherlock Holmes; but no such gift, in anything like that degree of development, is possessed by any detective I ever saw in any part of the world.

Detectives in many countries are men of very ordinary intellect who have started as policemen, and by showing a liking for the study—and sometimes the company—of criminals have been promoted to become professional spies, or "sleuths." Newspaper men cannot do as clever work as they where the case requires a knowledge of the faces, haunts, and habits of the evil-doers whom they pursue. It is when a crime is committed by some one not known to the police that the journalist and the detective are evenly matched, and then it is no wonder that the journalist often does better work than the policeman. It should be expected, I think. He is a much abler man, and would not deserve the credit he gives to himself were it not that he has to work unaided, if not obstructed, by the police, who usually deny him any credit when he has materially assisted them. Too many American detectives do their work by the aid of such criminals as can be found to betray their companions, and the assistance of the keepers of vicious resorts, who give secret information against their patrons in order to be protected, or unmolested, by the authorities.

I once knew an Irish detective who had read all the nonsense which has been written about

Vidocq, the great French detective, and who was thus inspired to make himself appear as subtle and mysterious as possible. Whenever he set out to go to a place he always started in the contrary direction and then turned and doubled on his tracks. Whenever he read a letter or a memorandum—even though it was only a bill from his shoemaker—he either chewed it up or burned it. If he saw a man let himself hurriedly or uncommonly quietly into a house at night he regretted that he could not take a room opposite the house and watch it for a few weeks. If his friends addressed him out loud by name on the streets he was very angry, and if a mere acquaintance saluted him he denied his identity. Of course, all these were mere monkey-shines, calculated to impress men of his own mental caliber. When he undertook the greatest piece of work in his career, which was to discover the assailant of a well-to-do woman in New York, he fixed the crime upon her husband, "because he and she had occupied separate apartments in their home."

Neither criminals nor police have ever attracted or interested me, and detective-reporting has taken little of my time, yet I have been obliged to give these people and subjects some attention, for the most part unavoidably. One of the most novel of my minor experiences was one which led many of my fellow-citizens to say that I saved an innocent person from a shameful death. It was a case of pitting cold logic against detective stupidity; for what milder term can I give to that too common habit with some police of making an arrest and then twisting and distorting evidence to fit the bird in hand, rather than acknowledge his innocence and set themselves the more difficult task of finding the real culprit. In this case a chemist in a great city employed a prescription clerk and an errand-boy.

The life and companions of the clerk were disgraceful, while the boy was a poor orphan who had worked hard and steadily from infancy without a blot upon his character. The clerk came to bed in his room in the rear of the shop at a very late hour one morning, and presently arose again to let in the boy, who reported at the proper hour. The boy immediately went out to buy his employer's breakfast, and while he was gone a neighbor walked in, heard an unaccountable noise of groaning, and found the clerk dying of wounds made by a hatchet which lay by his side. A few minutes later the boy returned, cool, frank of face and manner, and cleanly dressed in the only suit of clothing he possessed. Nevertheless, he was selected by the police to be charged with the crime, and for weeks he was put through every ingenious test and subjected to every trick—fair and unfair—which the police could invent to make him confess his guilt. Traps were set for him, detectives were locked up in his cell with him in the guise of fellow-prisoners, all that was known of the affair was distorted to apply to him, despite the fact that the dying man had said that "after the boy went out I stooped to tie my shoe and *a man* struck me." I owe it to Chester S. Lord, the managing editor of the New York *Sun*, to say that he gave me the commission, and was first stirred by the humane impulse to save the boy. I merely executed the task, and succeeded in freeing the lad by means of a calm two-column statement of the unquestioned facts. By concealment of some facts, and the distortion of others, the case against the boy had been made to appear convincing; but when the whole truth was massed candidly beside the unbroken good record of the prisoner's life, the police fabric fell to pieces like a house built of cards. The incident is worth mentioning because it shows that logic and sober sense may just as well be used to defeat the abuse of justice as in executing it; and, again, to be able to overthrow the plans of a wonderful body of officials with a mere report in a newspaper demonstrates the power of a journalist—that power which lends to his calling so much of its fascination.

If I once gained his liberty for a boy, it is but frank to admit that I, at another time, deprived a man of his. There had been a remarkable series of fires in a certain country region. Barns, sheds, even occupied farm-houses, had been mysteriously fired, and night after night the red glare of burning buildings increased the panic of a quiet community. I happened in the neighborhood one morning after some vagrants had been arrested upon the vaguest suspicion that one of them might have had a hand in the incendiarism.

As business with the sheriff took me to the jail, I went through that building. How or why I came to converse with the wretched prisoners, whose chief interest lay in the commonplace fact that they were vagrants, I do not know, yet I did so, and one, a negro, confessed that he was the "firebug" who had been terrifying the countryside. He was a feeble-minded creature, with an irresistible penchant for arson. He said that he confessed his crime to me because I was not a constable. He wished to ease his mind, but would not give the authorities the satisfaction of a talk with them. I made a bargain with the authorities by which I left them to obtain the confession anew for themselves (without obliging me to give testimony), while I secured what is called a "beat" for my paper—a "beat" being an exclusive piece of news, and the getting thereof being the highest aim and the proudest achievement of a correspondent.

To play the detective and be taken for the criminal is a mishap the like of which I have heard of only once, except when it happened to me. And then it gave me a shock as great as may be looked for even in the exciting career of a correspondent. The case of which I heard was that of an English journalist of note who, I believe, is an editorial writer rather than a correspondent, although on the occasion in question he was travelling and writing for an English newspaper. He had been in Berlin and had gained an idea that his friends in authority there were withholding important and disturbing information concerning the military doings of the Austrians. Something very like a war-cloud hovered above the borders of Austria and Russia, and he determined to go to the scene and judge for himself. He speaks German fluently, or one would be appalled to think what might easily have become his fate.

He went to a city on the Russo-Austrian border, and, stopping at a hotel merely long enough to drop his luggage, he hired a carriage and told the driver to go the rounds of the fortifications at the outer edge of the city. Coming to a point where the Russians were throwing up earthworks in front of the Austrian line, he saw a Russian officer and a small posse of men, and, thinking that a word with him might throw some light upon the situation, he leaped from the carriage, saluted the Russian, and exchanged two or three sentences with him. "It looks like business," he said, in effect. "Yes, it looks very like business," the Russian replied. The journalist did not suspect it, but he was being watched, and his actions appeared very suspicious. He returned to his carriage and drove back to his hotel.

At dinner that night the proprietor of the hotel came to him and whispered, "You are to be arrested in a few minutes, and I thought I would give you warning so that you might be prepared and not say or do anything thoughtlessly. You are taken for a German spy, but I believe you are an Englishman, and that the military authorities are mistaken." He was arrested and carried to the massive fortress of the place. Some perfectly innocent letters were found upon him, and tended to confirm the suspicion against him, because they were from high German officials. Worse yet, the telegram which he sent to his paper in England, asking his employers to vouch that he was their correspondent, was not answered. Telegrams to Berlin brought immediate assurances that he was a distinguished English journalist, but the governor of the castle said that this promptness and anxiety to befriend him were things to be expected, and were more damaging than helpful. The governor dined with the prisoner, who knew that he stood a very likely chance of disappearing from the sight of his friends without as much to mark his exit as the circles made by a pebble cast into a pond. He made the utmost of his opportunity to impress and interest his jailer. He was desperate. He talked all that dinner-time, and then talked harder over coffee, and finally kept the governor up hours after the meal was cleared away, nervously, excitedly going over every argument and statement he could devise to prove that he was merely a journalist who was looking out for "copy" for his paper.

On the next day the governor assured the other officials that he was convinced the prisoner stated the truth as to his identity and calling. The happy fellow was ordered out of town, and accompanied to the railway-station by a guard of soldiers, to make sure that the place was rid of his disturbing presence. The governor told him that but for his knowledge of the German tongue he could never have cleared himself, and must have been imprisoned.

That of which I speak as happening to me occurred in a widely different field, and was not carried far enough to be as serious as the London writer's mishap, yet there is a similarity between the cases. As I reported the affair to my own paper soon afterwards, "it was merely an episode in a reporter's life, one of those adventures which make the career of a newspaper correspondent the most exciting, the most picturesque, and one of the most hazardous in the multifarious roll of employments."

In this case a beautiful girl had been found dead by a road-side close to her home. The crime stirred the most populous part of the United States. Its mystery was absolute, and never yet has been pierced. The reporters of the press of several cities met at the scene and literally sifted the neighborhood for an inkling of the guilty. Night and day they worked, and night and day, as is so often the case, the police loafed about with garrulous solemnity, increasing in stupidity. I, for one, discovered facts which would have justified the arrest and trial of one of the deceased girl's neighbors, but the police could not be aroused to look into his connection with the case.

One afternoon, when I was at the house of the afflicted family, I had the adventure of which I write. The wretched people were very ignorant and superstitious. It seemed certain to them that the crime had been committed by some stranger. My enthusiastic interest in the case forced my personality upon their minds, and they fell into the mistake of doubting that I was a journalist and of suspecting that my interest in the case was of the sort that is often dwelt upon in fiction as compelling a villain to loiter near the scene or by the victim of his misdeed. The brothers of the murdered girl were street laborers. They were present, with a male friend or two. Their mother invited me into the dismal parlor, and all advanced to the side of the coffin except one brawny man, who stayed behind to close and guard the only door to the room. I had noticed a strange awkwardness in their behavior towards me, but suspected nothing, and accepted the invitation to view the body, first, because it was a natural thing for them to proffer, and, second, because I needed to know what fashion of woman the deceased had been. But now that I was in the room, and a prisoner, one of the burly brothers turned and said:

"Put your hand upon her."

"Yes, put your hand on the body," echoed another.

I realized at once that I was suspected of being the miscreant for whom all were searching, and that I was in the presence of one of the oldest and strongest superstitions that has taken root in ignorant minds the world over—the belief that a body will turn or its wounds will reopen if it is touched by the person who caused its death.

"Put your hand there."

"Nonsense; I don't want to," said I.

"You must do it," said the brawnier of the two brothers, with a look like a threat that he meant to use force.

I would have died before I would have done as he bade me.

"I will not do it," I answered. "I understand why you want me to, but I never saw your sister in life, and never was in this town until after her death. I am a journalist, and am known as such to many of my companions who are here. This is all nonsense, and I warn you to drop it and let me out of this room."

I turned quickly, and, walking to the man who guarded the door, fixed his eyes with mine, and in a tone of absolute mastery commanded him to let me out. He dropped his eyes and stood aside, and I walked out into air that tasted freer and fresher than I had ever known air to taste, though the same sensation has come upon me more than once since then in distant parts of the earth.

VI

The Mysterious Sixth Sense

AT one time my "chief," as we called the editor in supreme control of a newspaper, said that until further notice I might stay at home and amuse myself, as no news was stirring anywhere in the world. After what I think was the only week of absolute idleness I had known since leaving school, I started out one evening to see Sir Henry Irving in "Louis XI." I had gone about four blocks from my home, out of a quiet residence street into the boisterous stir of Sixth Avenue, in New York, when I saw a district messenger lad propelling himself head foremost, as boys and bullets have the way of doing. Something prompted me to put out an arm and stop him. "Where are you going with that message?" I asked.

"Ralph," said he; "19 West Thirty-eighth Street."

"Give it to me," I said, and he did so. It was a request from my office to know whether I could start the next morning at seven o'clock to fill the post of correspondent in London for my paper.

That was an operation of what I call the sixth sense of a journalist. None except newspaper men have it, unless detectives feebly share it with us, which I doubt, for detectives are distinctly a lower order of men, whose alleged feats of ratiocination and of judgment occur only in works of fiction. In real life, cunning is apt to be a high quality with them. This sixth sense of the journalists is by no means akin to the news sense. A newspaper man must have the news sense in order to distinguish what is worth publishing, and to know what proportions to give to the various incidents which make up a newspaper, if he be an editor, or which constitute the story he is writing if he be a reporter. He can get along very well without the sixth sense, which is a most mysterious quality or instinct, and which many possess, but no man can command or rely upon. It seizes a man with irresistible force and leads him to what he seeks. Sometimes it even takes him to the seat of news which he is not seeking and of the existence of which he has had no inkling. It frequently impels him to act against his judgment and to do things which he feels to be absurd, and yet is obliged to persist in until the reward comes with a shock like lightning from a cloudless sky.

But illustrations make the best form of explanation.

The morning on which Captain Dreyfus's lawyer, Maître Labori, was shot down on his way to the court in Rennes is fresh in every one's mind. In my own it is as clear as you may imagine when you learn that here, at Rennes, I am writing this at the same table and with the same pen that I used in describing the startling event. My alarm-clock was set for half-past five, yet, though I had not enjoyed a fair night's rest for a week, I could not sleep after five o'clock. I went to the court early, and on the way I passed the telegraph-office. "Will you wait a minute?" I asked my companion, Mr. G. W. Steevens, of the London *Daily Mail;* "I think I will telegraph my people that I expect exciting news to-day." I do not know what it was that prompted this. Perhaps the cross-examination of General Mercier, the bitterest accuser of Dreyfus, by Dreyfus's gigantic champion, was uppermost in my mind. Yet that did not require nor deserve a telegram of warning—in fact, there was no need at all for warning those who must always be prepared for great news. Nevertheless, the warning came to me, and the incident serves as a perfect example of the working of this strange sixth sense.

It is quite apart from common-sense, is this strange gift. Every man who falls under its influence may wish that such wise prompting could come to him in his private affairs and guide him in his daily walk, for each one of us who has benefited by these brilliant promptings in his business has done things in the course of his private affairs which after-events have proved to be stupid in the extreme. I, for instance, was once employed to write a book for a great syndicate. It turned out that my employer not only had no right to act for the people he said he represented, but he was, in addition, an extraordinary and notorious habitual criminal. The sixth sense might have told me this, saving me a deal of humiliation and giving me a startling piece of news, but it has never operated in my behalf in any except my journalistic affairs.

A former master of the science of journalism, Mr. John B. Bogart, who was both admired and beloved by all who worked under him, used to call the sixth sense a "current of news." He once said this to me:

"One day I was walking up Broadway, and had crossed Fulton Street, when suddenly a current of news came up from a cellar and enveloped me.

I felt the difference in the temperature of the air. I tingled with the electricity or magnetism in the current. It seemed to stop me, to turn me around, and to force me to descend some stairs which reached up to the street by my side. I ran down the steps, and as I did so a pistol-shot sounded in my ears. One man had shot another, and I found myself at the scene upon the instant."

But only think of the case of Mr. Balch, now the assistant of Mr. Kennedy Jones, the conductor of the *Evening News*, of London. Mr. Balch was in Boston at the time of a most sensational tragedy in New York. There was nothing ever so vague to connect any one in Boston with the extraordinary affair. On one evening Mr. Balch walked to or from his dinner in the streets of Boston and passed a colored man. He may have passed ten or even fifty others in the course of the same walk, yet on the moment that he saw this particular person he became seized with the idea that this might be the man whom the police of New York suspected of a dreadful part in the tragedy which engrossed their attention. He followed the man to—what do you suppose?—a church, of all places. He watched his behavior during the early part of the service. He saw the man exhibit to his female companion (or else he saw adorning the woman) some jewels like those by stealing which the man had added the sin of theft to his more hideous crime. He left the church and notified the Boston police of his discovery. Some officers returned with him to the church, and the end of it all was the arrest of Chastine Cox, the slayer of his benefactress, Mrs. Hull, in West Forty-second Street, New York. This man confessed his crime to me, and I might argue that he was forced to do so, and that I was obliged to obtain his confession for the New York public; but this was not due to any power we mortals cannot comprehend.

When the news of the arrest reached New York I went to an official of the police and stated my intention to accompany him to Boston. It was then midnight, and the first train left at six o'clock in the morning. I said that I was sure the official would take that train and would return with the prisoner on the Fall River boat the next night. At first he denied that he contemplated any such errand, and when I persisted in maintaining that he would go and that I would go with him he refused to allow me to be his companion.

"Any one can go who can pay his fare there and back," said I, "and I assure you I shall make the trip with you."

He succumbed to the force of logic and of circumstances, and I alone from among all the reporters of New York made the journey. On the return trip, aboard the steamboat, I sat up with the criminal all night, and heard the story of his crime repeated and repeated until I was able to write it out at the length of several columns. The adventure of Mr. Balch illustrates the working of the sixth sense. That which influenced me was the news sense—a widely different and easily explainable faculty or impulse.

Nothing in all my experience, perhaps, seems to me more inexplicable and extraordinary than another incident which occurred at about this same time. It was suspected that a clergyman must be in the possession of some sensational facts concerning a matter of acute public interest. He had but newly come to the city, his address was not in the directory, and no one could be found who knew him or anything about him. All that was known was that a clergyman had performed an important ceremony in connection with a case which was, in all other respects, likewise clothed with mystery. Moreover, if he should be found it was very likely that he would refuse to tell what he knew of the persons who had called for his ministrations.

I was "on the case," as the saying goes, and suddenly, as I was walking with another reporter in a section of the city which was removed from the sphere of our work, we saw a most unclerical-looking man walking along the opposite pavement. I said at once, as if another person had spoken with my lips:

"There is the clergyman for whom we are looking."

"He is not a clergyman at all," said my companion; "he is a country storekeeper or clerk."

At the same instant the man across the street turned, ran up a flight of stairs, and entered the door of a house. It was not such a building as one would expect a clergyman to enter, yet I ran across the street, while my companion called after me that I was unreasonable and was wasting valuable time. The door opened for me and I asked what person had sent for the clergyman, and to what part of the house he had gone. I ran to where I was directed, and came upon the object of my pursuit, who was so surprised and taken off his guard that he acknowledged having performed the ceremony about which I sought information, and, after that, was easily led to tell me all that I desired to know.

That was the work of the sixth sense, pure and genuine.

On another occasion which I recall, I was reporting the work of the Legislature in Albany, and it had become my delight to go to the beautiful park in that capital and look across a valley at the softly swelling purple mountains in the near distance, to the southwest of the city. Suddenly I was seized with an almost uncontrollable desire to go to the mountains and to witness the comparatively primitive life of the people there. During two days this impulse never left me, and on the third afternoon I read a ten-line paragraph reporting a peculiar occurrence in a hamlet upon those very mountains. The occurrence had taken place on the day I received the prompting. It was a paragraph which was the mere seed of suggestion of a notable story. It sent me speeding to that region, and I there obtained the material for an article which included a study of the people.

In that adventure one clearly distinguishes the two impulses apart from each other. The first urging proceeded from what, for the want of a better term, is here called the sixth sense. The second impulse was generated by the news sense. To make the difference still more clear, I may tell how once, when I was sent to Utah to report the resources of the country, I decided that if I could establish sufficiently close relations with the leaders of the Mormon Church it would be far more interesting and novel to make a close study of the character, habits, and aims of the Mormons, and to describe their homes, shops, and churches. I easily obtained the friendly interest of certain leaders, and abandoned my original purpose in going to their State. My news sense told me that this would prove far more generally interesting than a dreary summing-up of the annual production of grain, cattle, metals, and manufactures in that strange corner of the globe.

The two senses are absolutely distinct, though, as already stated, I suspect that the sixth sense is of use only to journalists. The existence of these mental guides will not be disputed by any practised newspaper man. All such are made aware by these instincts that it is impossible to teach young men and women to be journalists. You may teach the laws governing poetry, and clearly point out the almost divine element which enlivens the best poems, but that will not make poets of your pupils. No work upon war and no course of study can develop a Von Moltke; not even a designer of carpet patterns or of teaspoons can be trained to succeed except the impulse and the aptitude be in his make-up. This is why schools and classes of journalism are superfluous and nearly worthless. The real schools are the newspaper offices, and yet it is perfectly possible for the genuine journalistic talent to exist in persons who have never had to do with a newspaper or publication of any kind.

To illustrate what I mean by this, let me say that the best account of a shocking disaster in the English Channel last spring was written and despatched ahead of all the reports of the professional news-gatherers by a business man in London who was rescued from the vessel which foundered at sea. His first thought was to proclaim his safety to his friends at home. But by the time he reached a telegraph-office on the French shore, where he had been landed, he concluded to send a complete account of the disaster to a newspaper friend of his in London. He proved himself to possess every quality of a practised correspondent, though he had never before exercised his gifts in that way. He gave to the world the earliest news of the disaster, an explanation of what caused it, a picture of the shocking scenes which ensued, and the names of as many of the dead and the surviving passengers as he knew—all graphically set forth, and with the various features in their just proportions.

He had the gifts of narrative and of description, and he possessed the news sense. All that he lacked was the subtle sixth sense of which I have treated here. If he had possessed that gift, the layman's spirit within him would have met it thus: "That ship is going to be wrecked, or something dreadful is going to happen on the voyage. I will not sail in her." On the other hand, had he been a professional reporter or correspondent of the highest order he would have responded to the vague, uncertain warning with this thought: "Something tells me that I am going to get good 'copy' out of this voyage to-night. I wish the vessel would start at once. I wonder what I am going to run across."

VII

The War Correspondents

WHEN one thinks of the dangers which lie across the path of the journalist, the mind turns first to the war correspondent, and after that to the special or travelling correspondent whose work takes him among uncivilized peoples. They risk their lives so constantly and are so often in the public eye and mind that people generally must wonder what sort of men they are. I fancy that it must be a common belief that few men exist who would care to do their work, and that they are most likely to be reckless fellows, perhaps with a great deal of swagger and bounce about them. Nothing could be more remote from the truth. For every man in these branches of journalism there must be at least a hundred who long to do his work. Then, as to their temperament, they must be cool, clear-headed, sensible men. Necessarily, the more deliberate and prudent they are the more successful they are certain to be. Whether they are born so or whether familiarity with danger sobers them I do not know, but it seems to me that those who risk their lives most frequently in this calling are among the most modest, quiet, and sober fellows I have ever met with in any walk of life.

Every night, in the foreign city where I am now reporting, one hundred and fifty correspondents gather before the principal coffee-house, the only high-class rendezvous of the city, to enjoy their coffee and cigars and to gossip with one another. Three of these are distinguished war correspondents whose names are known to every journalist in England and America. All three expect to meet in the next war, whose signs of precipitation they discuss daily. They speak of reporting it precisely as if it were no more than a political meeting, except one, who fancies that it will be very hotly contested and bloody, and therefore says he expects "good copy" and "plenty to do."

The name of one of these men is associated with stirring adventure and hair-breadth escapes in both the Caucasus and the Balkans. He is the last one you would pick out for what he is in all the crowd. He works harder than any man there, and is the most retiring and undemonstrative among them all. He is the first to break away and seek his hotel of an evening, for it is his nature to like his own company best—a result of the years he has spent with rude peoples. In London or New York you might take him for a journalist, because the men of that calling are the only professional men who are not marked by any peculiarity of dress, manner, or appearance. But I should say he was an overworked book-keeper if I knew no better. The second man has led a long life of dangerous adventure on sea as well as on land. He is distinctly cosmopolitan. If you saw him walk into a hotel in Paris, London, San Francisco, or Bombay, you would say to yourself: "That is a citizen of the world. His nationality is effaced by the fact that he knows all countries." He walks in boldly, but without a trace of swagger. He chooses a seat, a friend drifts to his side, and after that you must bend close to him to hear what he is saying. If you ask him, he will tell you of his adventures, but always as if he were telling a story of what happened to another man. And what he lays stress upon will not be his courage or peril, but the comical side of the things he has known. When he tells you of being saved from shipwreck to be at once imprisoned as a spy, the point he dwells on with gusto will be this: that without a penny in his pocket he induced the governor of the jail to serve him with special fare, for which he paid when his employers learned of his plight. The last of the three men is by far the most brilliant writer. He has seen three campaigns and two wars, but you have to be told so, for he is so shy in his manner and so self-depreciating at most times that you might fancy he belonged in a small English town and was away from it for the first time in his life.

The manager of a London daily newspaper tells me that when the word goes out for the war correspondents to be ready to start upon a campaign, Fleet Street becomes the Mecca of scores, perhaps hundreds, of other men who want to get the same commissions. Many are journalists not regularly employed upon any newspaper, but a greater number are students, young barristers, and idle men of means. I have heard of their offering to work for nothing and pay their own expenses. I have heard of an actor, and again of a theatrical manager, who applied to be sent to a war. I have been told, too, that there are men in London who fly to the newspaper offices upon reading the merest hints or prophecies of trouble in other lands, saying: "Do you not think these may lead to war, and will you not remember that I have made the first application to be sent to it?" The moral of all this is that danger is not a deterrent with many men; in fact, danger is an incentive and an attraction to thousands. If courage were all that is required of a war correspondent, there would be so many to choose from that their pay would be very small. As a matter of fact, it is taken for granted that every correspondent has courage, and the tests are upon his other qualifications—his sagacity, his ability to write, and his persistence and enterprise in getting his reports through to his newspaper.

In China, during the war with Japan, there were no war correspondents on the Chinese side. The first time I ever saw these men at work was on the battle-ground before Domokos, in Thessaly. The battle had ended, the Greeks had fled, as usual, and the Turks were resting on the scene. A few large tents had been set up, and of two which faced one another, one was that of Edhem Pasha, the victorious leader, and the other was what one may call the *salle du correspondance* of the newspaper men. This tent contained no furniture. In it, upon the bare ground, eight or nine Englishmen and Americans were lying upon their stomachs or their haunches, writing their reports. A French-English dictionary lay among them, and was occasionally passed from one man to another, for it was required that our reports should be written in French, and not all the correspondents were good French scholars. Except that they wore revolvers, there was nothing peculiar about their dress or appearance. They wore flannel shirts, loose, short coats, and knickerbockers or riding breeches, and most of them would have passed muster in any small American town.

A pretty incident occurred while all were busy in getting off their accounts of the battle. A poor Turkish soldier with a gaping hole in his back at the base of his neck staggered along to the door of the tent. I had met a great many wounded Turks that morning, and had had them call to me from the bushes and depressions by the roadside. In every case they wanted cigarettes, and one or two asked for water as well. They had been exposed to the almost freezing night, and now were baking in a sun hot enough to bring out millions of poppy blossoms, which splotched the battle-fields as with blood. Like them, this man had been freezing, and now was baking, yet all he wanted was a cigarette. No one of them ever complained of his wounds. I wonder what the weakened, staggering chap thought as he saw the correspondents leap to their feet and make a back-rest for him with their coats, while some cut away his clothing and sponged and cleaned his wound, and others fetched him a stimulant, and still others ran for the English surgeon? To his Turkish mind it may have seemed as if he had fallen in with a lot of women in men's clothing; but he must have been glad in his heart, though he uttered no thanks.

My own experiences were amusing rather than serious. They all occurred in getting to and from the war. As an especial favor I was allowed to go part of the way in a freight-car, and, when two Turkish officers asked leave to share the hard and jolting floor of the car overnight, we made them welcome. They proved to be the most disagreeable human companions with whom I ever spent a night, for they quarrelled, and one kept drawing a fearfully big dagger and attempting to stab his companion with it. We only made believe to sleep, and watched them out of the corners of our eyes.

Arrived at the end of the railway, we managed to strike a bargain by which we loaned our horses to some officers in charge of a train of hackney carriages taken from the cabmen of Salonica for use as ambulance wagons. They gave us the right to ride in the carriages. Thus it came about that I was one of the first men who ever rode to war in a landau. Wherever we stopped for a night the richest Greek in the place was bidden to entertain me, and a Turkish soldier stayed in the house each time to see that the wretched people gave me plentifully of their best. It was pitiful to see these bankers and rich merchants routed out of bed and made to put on their best apparel and to cook our meals at midnight. Wives, servants, children—every one—had to be up and doing for us. Wonderfully lucky as it was to escape a night in a filthy Turkish khan, or tavern, the pleasure was marred by the knowledge that I was not cheerfully served or truly welcomed.

In the city of Larissa the governor gave to Mr. Roberts, of the Washington *Post*, and to myself and my son, the beautiful villa from which a Greek professor had run away on the approach of the Turks. As the front door was kicked in to save the time and trouble of unlocking it, we were at the mercy of thieves all the time. All Albanians are thieves, and a company of them was encamped beside the low wall of our garden.

True to their instincts, they made an attempt to rob us, but this only occasioned the most laughable incident of the entire campaign. They came while we were away and had left our house in charge of a moon-faced Turk who acted as our cook. He could not speak any language we understood, so he told us about it in pantomime, something after this fashion:

All is quiet—the house is in his charge—he is asleep in a chair with his head against a wall. Cr-r-r-ck! Pist! What's that? He wakes—opens his eyes—cocks his head on one side. Hark! He leaps to his feet—peers through the shutters—sees some Albanian bashi-bazouks climbing over the wall into our compound. They are thieves, ruffians, murderers! What is to be done? Ah, he knows! He throws open the window. He waves the men away. They hesitate. "Turque! Turque!" he cries (meaning, "This is a Turkish house; therefore one you dare not rob"). Pist! Cr-r-r-ck! They drop back again on the other side of the wall.

Never in any theatre in any part of the world have I seen an actor who did as clever a bit of playing as this man did in telling that story by signs. Every day and many times a day I made him repeat this story for my visitors—in reality, I did so in order that I might be sent into roars of laughter by his comical face and gestures.

At one point on our return from the war we bargained to be driven with our baggage to a certain railway station. We decided to alter our route afterwards, but the owner of the wagons and his men flatly refused to make any change in their plans. We had a very exciting time, and came very near seeing our belongings dumped on a mountain-pass and abandoned. By exercising patience and cunning we induced the men to proceed to a certain town, where we knew—but they did not—that the governor was our friend. When we got there our servants were told to obey us in all things or they would be severely punished.

They promised to do so, but ran away with all our property the moment we left the town. Thus we found ourselves in the middle of Macedonia without servants, baggage, or horses; in fact, we had nothing but the clothes we were wearing. That looked like a very serious adventure, but it amounted to nothing more than a day's worry. We reached the railway, took the train, and at the station to which our men had bargained to take our goods we found them and our property awaiting us. The worst feature of that experience was that by reason of it we were obliged to spend one night in a Turkish khan. My bed was a frame of wood with a sheepskin laid upon it. How many years that had been there without being cleaned, and how many peasants had slept upon it, I do not care to know. Within an hour after I had lain down upon it I began to suffer such torture that I almost feared I should be devoured before morning. From this misery I rescued myself by a very simple but most efficacious proceeding. There was in the room a lamp which held between a pint and a quart of kerosene. I opened the lamp, stood upon the sheepskin cot, and poured the oil all out upon my head. Then I put on my night-gown and lay down. My tormentors either died or imitated the Greeks in battle, I do not know which. But I lay down and enjoyed the sleep of the just.

A sad, and to us a melancholy, interest attaches to this subject, for the war correspondents of to-day are the last men who will ever serve in such a capacity. Two of the great nations have resolved to exclude them from their armies, and no one doubts that the others will do the same. Unavoidably, the correspondent supplies the enemy with news. After this he will only be allowed to report small affairs with savage tribes where Europe is concerned.

VIII

THE DANGERS OF WAR-REPORTING

IN speaking about the element of danger in the life of an active newspaper correspondent, I had a great deal to say about war-reporting. The mere fact that a reporter takes the greatest chances with his life when in the company of soldiers might easily lead to the thought that soldiering is more dangerous than reporting. It does not begin to be so dangerous. There is an English war-artist who has experienced more than two dozen campaigns, and therefore has seen more of war than any military officer or private in Christendom. Pryor and Villiers among the artists, Knight and Williams among the writers, are all many times more used than any soldier to the roar of cannon, the flash and crackle of rifle-fire, the crash of opposing forces, and the sight of the dead and wounded on the battle-field. Since it has come into fashion for the correspondents to ride out with reconnoitring parties, to take part in small skirmishes, and to get as close to, or as deep into, the main battles as they can, the life of the correspondent has become extra-precarious. In one of the great London dailies the other day I read this comment upon the life of a British soldier:

"Mr. Wyndham appears not to have seen any active service, but that is true of most soldiers; and the private who gets as much as six months' campaigning during his years in the army is fortunate indeed. Nearly the whole of every soldier's time is simply spent in routine —washing, dressing, cleaning, bed-making, drills, guard, and meals. It is a necessary and highly improving routine, but, apart from the sentiment of the thing, there is almost as much romance and excitement in a housemaid's life."

Since every word of this is true, how startlingly it presents the contrast between the deadly, dull, mechanical routine of the average European soldier and the almost meteoric, continuously hazardous, ever-straining career of a great reporter of to-day!

When I told of the unlooked-for number of Englishmen who are forever clamoring to be sent to report whatever war either goes on or is merely threatened, I did not mean, by inference, to leave my own countrymen in any less advantageous light—if love of risk and adventure be a thing that glorifies a man. When the war between the

United States and Spain broke out there were more candidates for the spurs of fighting correspondents than ever were seen or heard of in the world before. Those who were chosen and who went to the front or to the various camps numbered hundreds, and double as many were disappointed. I recommend every prospective journalist to read the account of Mr. Frederic Remington of his experiences in the campaign before Santiago de Cuba if he wants to know the reverse side of the picture which allures so many men. The article appeared in *Harper's Magazine* for November, 1898. The reality of campaigning in a hostile climate, without the rudest comforts or the necessaries of life, is set forth with naked candor. It was such a change from the excitement of marching behind a band, amid the plaudits of the multitude, in streets festooned with bunting, that many a man who had no lack of valor was none the less sick of his experience.

A good story about two well-known correspondents has drifted from Santiago into my notebook—a mere phrase, by-the-way, for I keep no diary. When the two first met in that war they were within range of the Spanish sharpshooters, but this they did not know. Both were stout men—noble and easy targets for the enemy, especially as the yellow road on which they met threw their dark forms into the boldest relief.

"Why, hello!" said one.

"Hello, ——," the other replied.

"Where are you going?" the first to speak now asked.

Crack! Crack! two shots rang out. Ping! Ping! sang two bullets as they spatted the road.

And the brave correspondents—what of them? Each one, by a common impulse, flung himself face down upon the road and rolled off its edge into a deep ditch of mud and water.

"Killed them both!" the sharp-shooters must have said, joyously, to one another, for that was how the extraordinary conduct of the two men must have explained itself.

A companion story to that—and a better one —was told me by Frederic Villiers when we were on our way to Japan in 1894. He was talking of his experiences in one of the early Soudan campaigns, and he said that on the morning in question he was taking an Englishman's constitutional, though on horseback, on the desert. Suddenly he saw two mounted natives circling, like eagles about to swoop down upon their prey, in the distance. It was he who was their intended prey. When they thought themselves close enough they began to fire their guns at him. He hesitated for a moment, then turned his horse's head towards them, jabbed in his spurs, and rode furiously at them. His only weapon was an empty pistol, but he brandished that ferociously, and raced like a madman straight for them. It was now their turn to hesitate, but after a moment they caught the reverse of the contagion of his courage and fled like frightened rabbits.

However, the truth is that most persons exaggerate the dangers of war to a correspondent. Sometimes they are unavoidably great and numerous to every person engaged in the farthest confines of the field of battle, but more often the greatest dangers are those which the correspondents make for themselves—especially now that they fancy themselves called upon to jeopardize their usefulness to the public and to strain the conditions laid down for non-combatants, on which, alone, they are admitted to an army.

My own experiences in war have been too slight for me to class myself with the brave fellows who follow it for a livelihood, and yet my calling has had its own frequent excitements in many and varied fields. The moral I have drawn from my own experience is that the greatest dangers always show themselves where they are least expected. The only man who ever tried to shoot me was a companion at a dinner-table. He was a Southerner—a South-Carolinian—and was incensed at my singing—but no; this would not be extraordinary: any one might reasonably show displeasure at that. On the contrary, he was angry, not at my singing, but at what I sang. It was the national air of his country and mine, but he said that unless I sang the "Flag that Bears a Single Star" he would kill me when he had counted three. I felt myself as good as dead, for I did not know either the words or the tune which he demanded. He levelled his pistol, counted o-n-e, counted t-w-o, was about to say t-h-r— when the man who sat nearest to him disabled him with a blow and saved my life.

At another time when Frederic Remington and I were on a deer-hunting trip in West Virginia we fancied that we had a Pullman car to ourselves, and sat cosily together in the smoking-room, enjoying the mountain scenery. Like an apparition, but of what Shakespeare calls "too, too solid flesh," there appeared between us a raving, frothing maniac, wild-eyed, excited, and stalwart. He began by asking Mr. Remington if he thought he was crazy, and with regret I record the fact that my friend said he had never seen a man more evidently sane.

"Of course," the maniac replied, "I'm sane as can be, but I'll kill my wife before they get me back in the asylum again. That's all I want. I'm going for her now, and I intend to cut her into mince-meat, because it was she who had me put away. I've just escaped from the asylum this morning, you see."

We agreed with all of his opinions and approved of all his murderous projects until we came to the first station, which happened to be the one at which we were to alight. Then we left him to hunt up the porter in charge of the car. And all that day we shook the West Virginia woods with laughter as we thought of the porter alone in that coach with the madman, frightened out of his five senses, and perhaps locked up in his little linen closet.

It is the unexpected that always happens, and he who misses death in a dozen wars may find it in a brick that topples from a chimney when, at his home, he fancies himself most safe. There can be nothing more prosaic in the way of extended travel in these days than a trip on a Cunarder across the Atlantic, and yet, less than a year ago, when I stepped out of the door of the smoking-room aboard the *Etruria* to see the appearance of the weather before turning in, a wave which swept the deck like lightning caught me and carried me away. First it wrestled with my knees while I held on to the knob of a door.

Then it seized my waist and threw me straight out at right angles to the door, to which I still clung. Finally it wrenched me loose and carried me away. Fortunately, the water lowered in depth as it ran, and therefore it was not able to lift me over the ship's rail. Instead, it hurled me against a great iron block in the stern of the ship. My feelings remain the most notable feature of the affair in my recollection, for the taste of death was strong upon me, and I did not mind it—so surely does Nature almost always prepare us with tenderest mercy for even our most shocking endings. This whole occurrence lasted less than sixty seconds, and yet it left me so exhausted that, as I sped along to what I thought was certain death, I lost all fear and care. I realized that I was lost, that I had no strength left with which to make a futile fight for life among mountainous waves in inky darkness, and with a warm, balmy, comfortable feeling of resignation I regarded death kindly; indeed, I would not have put out a hand to stave it off. I have a home and wife and children, and I am no callous man about these treasures, yet I never gave them a thought.

I once had a taste of nasty adventure upon a glacier in British Columbia, but the tale of that is not pertinent here because when I had it I was seeking what I got — an experience. But when at last I reached the moraine at the side of the glassy monster, my relief on feeling the great rocks beneath my feet was delicious enough to pay twice over for my previous shock. And then—then—in the very triumph of my new-found security I stepped upon a rock of the size of a farm-laborer's hut—and it began to roll over under me. It had been delicately poised upon a point of its surface, and my comparatively little weight was sufficient to start it anew upon the destructive course it had begun perhaps before the dawn of human history. I ran to one edge and then to another, and finally I lay down upon the monster, when, for my good-fortune, it came to another protuberance and rested again. So there was nothing in that adventure, after all—though I rank it among the most terrible I ever experienced, simply because it came immediately atop of a wild and exhausting moment of greater danger.

But with the knowledge of an adventure of my friend Captain Ahern, of the United States army, it does not become me to make much of any mere flirtation with danger. Captain Ahern was leading an exploring expedition in western Montana, and when one night he pitched his camp in the mountains, he walked out upon a glacier that lay on his route to see how he should dispose of his force in crossing it. It was after sundown, and the surface was hard and crusted and rough, so that it was evident that his men, mules, and horses could cross it as easily as any to follow any trail that led to where they were going. The captain saw below him, down the sloping, icy plane, a great crevasse, or fissure, capable of engulfing his entire little band, but so favorable were all the conditions that he was able to walk down to its menacing edge and stare into its darkening, icy depths.

On the next morning he and his men breakfasted and then made ready for the continuance of their march. The captain was the first to step from *terra firma* to the surface of the great river of ice. Lo! all the conditions of the glacier as he had found it on the previous night were changed. The surface was melting, slippery, with a shallow coating of water, and more insecure than polished plate-glass. The captain pushed ahead a few feet, and then his boots slipped and he found himself flung face down and flying along the sloping field of ice. He tried to dig in his toes and to catch himself with his finger-nails, but every effort was futile, and down and down the slippery mass he sped like fury. From the instant that he began to slide he thought of the crevasse, and all his effort was put forth to save himself from falling into it, for that meant certain and speedy as well as awful death. With the maddest energy he dug in his toes and scraped the ice with his fingers, but he still shot on and down, until at last some protuberance offered itself and his motion was arrested. He found himself clutching a knob of rough ice with his toes at the edge of the crevasse. After that he had to exercise his wits to direct the ignorant men in his command from cannonading their own bodies down upon him and forcing him as well as their own brave selves into the gaping jaw of the glacier. At last, following his commands, they rescued him. And what do you think was the first thing he did when he was back safe in camp? He called for a looking-glass. He says he wanted to see whether his hair had turned white. He saw that it had not, and then—if I remember aright—he fainted!

IX

The Importance of Good-Nature

IT does not seem that any one needs to be assured of the value of good-nature both as a shield against the kicks of fate and as a spur to the enjoyment of this world's blessings. Every man, and certainly every traveller, has found that a good temper or a kindly humor has bridged some very unpleasant breaks in the even tenor of his way. I remember breakfasting one day in Calgary, in the northwest provinces of Canada, when it was a very new town, and hearing an Englishman complain of finding no wash-bowl and pitcher in his room.

A very "tough" and desperate-looking waiter led him to a room in which there were a wooden trough, a water-bucket, and a towel. He said to him: "If that ain't a good enough place for you to wash in, why, you needn't to wash, d'ye see?"

When the Englishman came to the table he complained again, this time of the quality of the beefsteak which was served to him.

This was more than the insolent and acutely sensitive waiter felt called upon to endure, so he said, "Look here, that's the steak you git, and that's the steak you're going to like; now, you eat it and like it, d'ye understand?"

The man could have knocked the waiter down, but he would probably have been shot or roughly handled by the waiter's friends, but by ignoring the offence and behaving good-naturedly he made himself seem, what he really was, the lout's superior.

In the Kootenay country, in Canada, I stopped at what was sometimes called the "Hello Hotel," and also sometimes the "Telephone House," because only the frame and outer walls were up. There were no boards on the floors, and you could stand in any room in the house and order what you wanted from the office by calling down between the floor beams.

The barber in that hotel liked to boast of his depravity and to be considered a hardened and desperate character. He told me about himself while he was shaving me. Whether he was entirely jocular or partly mad I don't know, but he kept on accusing me of being afraid of him.

"I'm dreadfully afraid," said I, "but you see I am perfectly helpless. You have got me tucked into this chair, and I'll have to stand whatever you choose to do. Have it over quickly; that's all I ask." This amiable indifference puzzled him more than any course I could have adopted.

I put good-nature among the absolute essentials to success as a newspaper correspondent or reporter. It is one of the three main necessaries. First comes aptitude for the profession; next comes unconquerable persistence, or "stick-to-it-iveness"; and, third, good-nature.

My travels in China now seem to me the most enjoyable journeys I ever made, but had I not been armed with good-nature I might easily have been mobbed several times and possibly killed. We rested at a village one day while our servants were restocking our boat with provisions, and Mr. Weldon and I went ashore. I took with me a very stout walking-stick, which was the only weapon I ever carried out of the boat—in which we kept our guns and pistols.

I took the stick for frequent use against dogs, but I will not say here and at this time that I did not suspect a possibility of trouble with angry Chinamen as well.

The neighborhood was disturbed by an anti-missionary movement, but of this we had not been warned. The men of the village followed and watched Mr. Weldon and me, but kept well apart from us until at last we were in the thick of the houses and surrounded by the people.

Then one of the head men boldly advanced, backed up by a crowd, and, touching my stick, made motions as if to ask if it was not intended for Chinamen's heads. We were by this time well aware of our danger, but I dispelled it in an instant.

"No, no," I replied, by means of motions; "it is to hit dogs with."

This idea I conveyed by snapping and snarling and barking, while I laid about me, right and left, with my stick. At the end I laughed, and, as I expected, all the Chinamen laughed with me. They were all my friends from that instant, and the only trouble I suffered was from being obliged to repeat my pantomimic explanation ever so many times before I left the place.

Under more exciting circumstances I once lost my temper, but only for an instant and without evil consequences. Unless the reader has been in China and seen a great water-side city, like Canton, or many lesser places, he cannot imagine how crowded together and how numerous are the boats that are to be found there. We speak of "forests of masts" at London, Liverpool, and New York, but in China these are much more than forests—they are jungles.

At one large wholly Chinese port we were wriggling and twisting our boat along an ever-changing, constantly closing passage through one of these cities of water craft. Our captain was making the most of his dignity and his chance to display it. Few Chinamen have ever commanded a European vessel—or "glass boat," as it is called—because its windows are not of shell or paper like Chinese windows. He was yelling at every one ahead to get out of the way of his wonderful and majestic craft, and coupling with his commands the most violent and contemptuous abuse of whoever happened before us.

Suddenly, through clumsy steering on the part of the helmsman, our boat jostled a mandarin's gorgeous and towering floating house and did a dollar's worth of damage to a board on the side.

Instantly the mandarin's people leaped on our deck and laid hands on our captain. With equal promptness I rushed forward to drive or even throw them off our boat. My boy begged me not to interfere.

"The others are right," said he. "Our captain is to blame. He has enjoyed his boasting and abuse of every one. Now he must pay for his pleasure."

Had I struck a blow while embedded in the heart of a dense thicket of Chinese boats, it is not pleasant to think what would have happened. My captain was taken prisoner and held in pawn on the mandarin's boat, to be released when he had chaffered over the sum to be paid and had obtained the money. The absurdity of the situation and the awful fall of the captain from his proud position amused me, and I laughed heartily. Instantly my thousands of threatening enemies began to laugh with me. They became my friends and admirers.

I rank a laugh above money in China — far above firearms as a protection; high beyond any power that a white traveller can bring to his aid in an emergency. A light heart, a kindly bearing, and a merry spirit will grease a foreigner's way anywhere in China.

One day Mr. Weldon and I met a large section of the Chinese army hurrying to the war with Japan. A Chinese army in motion can be likened to nothing more truly than a flight of locusts. This one went as it pleased, not along any road, but spread out over a wide swath.

When it passed through a city it swarmed over the walls and into the gardens and houses, robbing and despoiling whatever lay in its path, and spreading terror even farther than it spread itself. It was an army in blue cotton, with tawdry banners which were as apt to be trailed downward as to be carried properly. The soldiers had guns, but they also carried sun-umbrellas and worked fans as they dog-trotted along.

We met them in a singularly lonely country which had been devastated in the Taiping rebellion. In all that desert of ruined and deserted towns and abandoned fields there were few persons but these soldiers, who seemed beyond the control of their officers. Now a "glass boat," such as ours, is always thought to be manned by English hunters and well fortified with firearms, so that it would naturally remain unmolested even by the rag-tag and bobtail element which serves China as her army. But my boy, on being visited by some officers, went out of his way to say that we were peaceable gentlemen, without any firearms, for on that one occasion we were travelling unarmed.

We soon discovered what this precious fool had said, and the rapid flight we made, with sail and oars and poles all working at once, was as ignominious as the subsequent retreat of that same army from its Japanese foes. We sped away all night, and I shall always think it was well that we did.

At another time we ran away "to live to fight another day." We carried many pounds of English candies, hard as bullets and put up in bottles. These we distributed, a few candies at a time, to the children wherever we went. One day as we sat in the boat's saloon at luncheon with our vessel moored to the shore, a large number of peasants came and squatted on the bank to see us eat. Our knives and forks and glasses and explosive bottles of bubbling soda-water interested them immensely.

"Hi! Yah!" they exclaimed; "how strange is everything the foreign devils do!"

It happened that our cook prepared an extra large pudding on that day, a rich preparation of marmalade and méringue, for we lived like nabobs and maintained nine servants upon something like four dollars a day. I rather think it cost less.

I asked Weldon to give me his share of the pudding, and then I went out with the dish and a long spoon and I fed that crowd.

The men wanted the women to try the pudding first, whether out of gallantry or a desire to see whether they would be poisoned I cannot tell. The mothers in their turn motioned for their babies to take the first spoonfuls. Finally they all took their turns, and I literally had to scrape the dish to satisfy them.

The pudding gone, Weldon and I sat out on the deck, and I remember how pleased I was with myself.

Presently Weldon remarked, "Just suppose

what would happen if one of those people should chance to have a stomach-ache." I turned that suggestion over in my mind, and the more I thought about it the less I liked it. In fifteen minutes we were in full flight again with all our men straining every muscle to leave that region far behind.

When I think of how I once bought the trousers of a village maiden in China it seems to me that it would be difficult to manage ever to do a more perilous or a more foolish thing. As all Mr. Weldon's pictures were painted in colors, he was obliged to purchase many costumes, and on this occasion he vowed it would be impossible to reproduce the uncommon and exquisite blue of this girl's trousers unless he could have them before him in his studio.

My boy, at whose laziness I was already vexed, declared that such a thing as purchasing the clothing of a person while it was in actual use was absolutely impossible. To shame him I ordered one of the sailors to make the purchase. He refused, and then it became obligatory upon me to perform the feat myself or lose my standing with my servants. In China one had better abandon his travels than lose his caste, or "face," as they say, with his inferiors.

Therefore I set out in a small boat on the Grand

Canal and followed the maiden to the home of her father. Before her wondering people I smilingly and yet very earnestly bargained for half of her attire—all in pantomime. My signs were greatly assisted by the ostentatious display of a Mexican dollar.

At last the maiden nodded "Yes," and, going in-doors for a few minutes, returned with the garment neatly folded. Triumphantly I went back to the boat and assembled my men to witness my success, and to warn them that thereafter they must know that to Americans nothing is impossible.

Only a day later Mr. Weldon paid a dollar to a peasant woman to remain in her water-side garden while he sketched it. Her husband found her thus employed and said to her: "You simpleton, would you sell your life for a dollar? If that man makes a sketch of your face your life becomes his to do with as he likes. At any day when he is gone and is across one of the four seas he may take up your picture and say, 'I wish this woman ill,' or 'I wish this woman to break her leg,' or 'I wish this woman to die a miserable death,' and whatever he wishes will that moment happen to you."

"Hi! Yah!" she screamed, and, flinging the dollar to the artist, scampered in-doors.

I sometimes think that the fun reporters get

out of their experiences is kept too much to themselves. Too few of us are like Charles Dickens, who crowded the zest and fun of his observations and adventures into even the most trifling things which his pen threw off. We seem to think that the public will not care to hear of the amusing happenings in our workday routine, but I believe this is a great mistake. Let me tell of a thing that happened only so long ago as the trial of Captain Dreyfus. Three news associations which were competing, were determined to beat one another in getting the first news of the verdict out to the world at large. When the final day came the manager of each association remained in the street to see that his reporter shot a message down a tube from the court-room to a messenger boy who waited outside to get it and bring it to the manager. All the rest of the correspondents saw these managers and messengers lurking in the street, and noted that the association reporters were in their places in the court-room, but all were so busy that they could not watch for the result of the intense contest in the feverish moment of the delivery of the verdict. They were obliged to wait until nightfall, when their own work was done, and then ask each of the managers how he came out in the race.

To our surprise, all three were desirous of

avoiding the subject, and yet, when they felt obliged to speak, each claimed the victory. "I got to the telegraph first with my despatch," said Mr. C. "Mine was the first to reach home," said Mr. V. "I don't believe I was beaten," said Mr. N. Not a word more would any one of them say.

The next day the whole truth came out. To appreciate the full extent of its drollness the reader must understand how intensely earnest the men were, how long and carefully they had planned to win, and how much it meant to the one who served his company's subscribers ahead of all the world. Mr. C. was the first to be "out with the truth," as he expressed it. He had hired a very bright, quick boy, and had trained him to be able to act in various ways according to the nature of the verdict. The boy had some large envelopes of different and pronounced colors, one of which symbolized "innocent," another "guilty," another "not proven." The boy was to hold up the envelope which stood for the verdict which would come to him in a message down the chute in the court-room window.

It was a good plan, well thought out, but it failed because the boy disappeared. Mr. C. waited until many men and boys had passed him, and then he obtained the news from some one else's boy and rushed to the telegraph-office, getting there ahead of every one. He has not yet seen his own messenger. He has been told that when the verdict was announced there was a mad rush of men to the chute, and a little boy was knocked down and trampled under many feet. He believes that boy and his are identical, but he can never be certain.

Mr. V. also hired a bright and active lad, and him he trained for the crucial moment at the chute. His boy was to hold up his right hand for "innocent," his left hand to signify "guilty," and both hands if the verdict was a Scotch one. With one hand or the other or both upraised, the boy was to speed like mad towards Mr. V., and Mr. V., seeing him from afar, was to turn and run to the telegraph with the verdict he could thus read at a glance. Alas! this shrewd and simple plan also went wrong.

Mr. V. waited, the verdict was delivered, the rush of men and lads ensued—and no boy with a hand held high in air was to be seen. Mr. V. saw boy after boy pass him, and his heart sank as one's heart must do when he sees himself beaten through no fault or failure of his own. Still, he stood and waited, and while he strained his eyes over the hurrying throng which filled the street, he felt a pull at his sleeve. He looked down, and there was his boy with both arms hanging by his side. "Why don't you have one hand up?" "I beg your pardon, sir; I forgot all about it." "What is the verdict?" "*Coupable*," said the boy in his native language, and away sped Mr. V., reaching the telegraph-office in time to push his despatch in next after that of Mr. C. What happened to Mr. N.—the third competitor—he would not say, but I imagine he reached the telegraph-office far behind the others. This doesn't matter now, for his telegram was received thirty minutes ahead of those of both his rivals! In spite of all their efforts, after their telegrams had been handed in the clerks sent them to be counted, and when this was done the topmost one became the one at the bottom, and the man who was first in the race was last in the result.

I have done very little reporting in London, except of great events like Mr. Gladstone's funeral and the Diamond Jubilee, yet I got sufficient amusement out of one experience to tincture a year of dull work with the pleasure of its memory. I was looking for a young woman whose career had brought her into momentary fame. The quest led me into strange halls and haunts and homes in Battersea.

One place that I visited was a decent, tidy, two-story dwelling in a bare, treeless street—one of those monotonies of brick and leaden skies that ought not to be in any Christian city in these enlightened days. Into the best room in this tidy tenement I was noisily welcomed by a round and red-faced man of the labor-agitator type, who said that he neither could nor would tell me anything, as his wife would return presently, and he always left "hall matters to 'er, speshully matters of himportance, like reporters and—and—such things."

When I was seated he began to walk around and around me, and to put absurd and not altogether inoffensive questions to me, such as "'Ow comes hit that you 'ave such fine clothes while Hi'm in 'omespun?" "I don't doubt you live in a fine 'ouse in the West End and 'ave your servants and your champagne, while honly look at me, obliged to in'abit this 'ere dog-'utch."

It seemed to me that he fancied himself with me on a platform at a laborers' meeting, and that he imagined the applause of his auditors as they heard his points pressed hard against me, while I was to be considered as shrinking and quivering with the guilty knowledge that I had not earned my good clothes, and should, by rights, be living in another "dog-'utch" like the rest.

"I 'ope you're not taking it 'ard for me to arsk these questions," he said.

"No," said I; "I think you are very amusing."

"Amusing!" he shouted; "that's what the gentry thought when the French Revolution broke hout; per'aps the wicked was amused when the Deluge began; maybe them as deals in 'uman flesh and 'uman 'earts, and widows' tears and sighs, will find it amusing when the day of reckoning comes in Lon'on."

"Hello!" I thought; "this is indeed a tremendous fire-eater, and the first I've seen in England."

Just then the man's wife came—unexpectedly and hurriedly, without warning of any sort. And what, think you, did this boastful and ferocious champion of oppressed manhood do?

He gave her a timid, frightened glance, snatched up a woman's apron, tied it around his waist, dropped upon one knee, and began to mend the fire in the grate.

"Don't blime me, dear," he pleaded; "I 'adn't forgotten the fire; really I 'adn't, my dear."

X

A Wide Field of Action

IN this chapter I propose to continue my own often amusing, usually non-commonplace, and sometimes risky adventures. I tell of my own because these are the ones I naturally know most about, though the life of any correspondent which covers as many years is apt to have been just as full of incident. Such a chapter has its place in this series because, as these haps and mishaps of a newspaper correspondent's life come trooping and crowding to the mind, one is able to see how wide a field and varied a collection of peoples, subjects, and situations are covered in the experience of the modern knight-errant. The modern knight-errant! How strange it is that we are able to-day to find a genuine and an ancient knight of romance, left over from the Middle Ages, with which to compare the men of the modern school!

We all of us felt refreshed by the appearance among us in this late century of a man like the disreputable Major Esterhazy, in the Dreyfus case. Leaving out his morals, which would not have been weighed in the age where he belongs, and regarding only his profession and experiences, we see that this extraordinary relic might easily, in mediæval times, have been a very notable, even a heroic, figure. With only his wits and his sword to live upon, he has drifted over Europe, serving in this army and that army and the other, now plotting with his superiors, now manœuvring for his own advantage, but often fighting, and always ready and eager to risk his life in battle or in duel. He has ended his career as a leading figure in a case almost as conspicuous as the sun-blaze, but it is ended only because of the age in which his part was played. In earlier centuries the wickedness of his part would not have been exposed, and we should have known only of his soarings—never of his stoopings. But there he stands—adventurer, knight, warrior, courtier, wit—a full reflex of a life which in its own proper period would have seemed all romance. And how does he compare with a knight of the pen to-day? How cribbed and confined does such comparison make his life appear; how narrow his field, how thin, sparse, and infrequent have been his adventures; how barren of good and of power appears his influence when contrasted with that which attends the exciting career of a first-class correspondent of to-day—especially of one who works only for the right, the truth, and justice, and will not pen a single word that does not rhyme with his convictions.

In the last chapter you were in China with me. Let us stay there a brief time longer. We shall get little of hair-breadth 'scapes or thrilling episodes, but we shall see ourselves far from Fleet Street, at least, surrounded by novel stage-settings. The Tao-ti, or Governor, of a city has had my Chinese passport presented to him, and for some reason takes its high-flown Oriental language literally—as if he were not used to the effervescence and flower of his own speech. He has sent word that he wishes me to dine with him, and I am on my way to his palace (?). Upon the drawbridge over the moat beside the wall are many lepers and other mendicants exhibiting the cruel ravages of hideous diseases. One of them has died overnight, and his body lies among the living, no one daring to touch it lest he be called upon to explain the cause of the man's death. "One piecee man makee die," says my interpreter, and that is all he thinks or cares about the matter. So we pass on under the arch and through the wall into a bustling Chinese city, where the entire four hundred millions of Chinamen appear to have come together. The long, narrow street is lined on either side with tiny shops which appear like holes in the wall and which fully reveal the interior crowds of workmen, salesmen, merchants, servants, and customers. Women and babies clutter the doorways, and bowls of burning charcoal stand on the counters to afford lights for those who smoke. The goods on sale hang all over the sides and ceilings of the shops and lie in heaps on the floors. The workmen make before your eyes many of the goods that you may be seeking to buy. The air above you at either side is cluttered with gaudy hangings and projecting signs, and every shop has its complement of lanterns. The street is all but blocked with chattering Chinamen in cotton clothes and often all but noiseless shoes, and these are pushed and knocked about by the bearers of burdens balanced on poles across their shoulders and by the rushing chair-bearers, who trot up and down carrying their masters and mistresses in silken-sided sedan-chairs. We pass a beautiful tea-house built on an island in a lake, and stop to see on the ground beside us a conjurer more wonderful than I have ever seen in London, New York, or anywhere in India. At last we reach the Tao-ti's palace. Its gate is what was once a beautifully designed portal of *arabesquerie*, but it is broken, unpainted, and shabby. We enter it and observe that at one side is a wall, and opposite that is a series of open buildings or pavilions. First is the guard-house, then beyond a court is the magistrate's court-room, then there is another open place, and last of all is the mandarin's dwelling. That, of course, is in three parts—a building for the men, another for the women, and the third for the servants. Thus for the first time we understand the Biblical expression, "In my Father's house are many mansions."

On the wall facing all these buildings is a huge painting of the tiger which was so inflated with vanity that it tried to eat the sun and got itself burned up in consequence. This is always painted where a magistrate or man of authority must see it in order to warn him of the necessity for modesty, self-control, and a due estimate of his own insignificance. We pass the lounging guards of the first pavilion—so like the loaferish Tammany parasites at home. Next we come to the prison, before which some prisoners are in boxes precisely like the wooden ones in which young canary-birds are carried, except that in this case the birds are in blue cotton and the cages are larger. Other prisoners sit or stand with their heads thrust through great squares of wood. We look into the jail for a moment and see all the prisoners in wooden cages — queer - looking, but, after all, not different in principle from our own prison cells. At last we come to the Tao-ti seated in ceremonial dress behind a table in a room with unheeded mottoes from Confucius and warnings against bribe-taking and corruption hanging about the walls. On the floor his retainers have flung in heaps the banners, fancy dresses, and antique weapons they carry before him when he goes out. The litter and disorder destroy the best efforts of the man to maintain dignity and impress us with his importance.

And now he leads us into the banqueting-hall in his mansion. A table is heaped with Chinese delicacies displayed on costly porcelain. Flowers, feathers, bronze, and crystal deck the snowy table. Beside it the whole front of the house is of glass, and against the glass every nose in the place is flattened. All his retainers are going to watch whatever goes on inside. There can be no privacy, no secrecy in China. Exclusiveness and aloofness would at once lead to suspicions of evil-doing—and suspicion in China is practically as bad as conviction. Before we eat we must undergo ceremony. The mandarin betakes himself to a high sofa, begs me to seat myself beside him, crosses his legs like a tailor, and commands his pipe. His secretary and distinguished friends arrange themselves like more tailors on other settees. Then the mandarin assures me of my greatness and asks to see the button of my rank. I can show no button, and neither he nor his friends can understand why. During the two hours I spend in that company the subject constantly recurs. It is no use for me to say that even my President, the ruler of my country, has no button of rank, for they think there cannot be rank without a button to distinguish it. One other remarkable difference between China and the West is brought out in our talk, and this time it is I who am puzzled.

"There is a war between you and the 'Little Black Men,'" I say, referring to the Japanese.

"Yes," says the mandarin, "and the Emperor has asked us for soldiers to help the North to fight the Little Black Men. We shall send no soldiers. If the North has got into a war, let it get out of it, I say. It is no concern of ours."

I remember one morning I awoke in my glass boat and came out on deck to breathe the fresh, clear air. We had moored our boat in the darkness, but daylight showed us a gate in a city wall just beside us. Suddenly some soldiers came swarming on the wall, some with bugles and some with guns. They dragged a cannon or two to the embrasures and pointed the muzzles down towards our little craft. My! but I was nervous when

I saw this. I sent my boy in haste to find out why we were about to be blown to kingdom come in this extraordinary way, without a chance to explain, apologize, or escape. The boy came lounging coolly back. "It is nothing at all," said he. "Soldier man hab take in cannon and gun in night so can go sleep. In morning soldier man bring out cannon, gun, banner, everything, so can watch, keep away bad people." And that was all it was.

And now we will, with one leap, betake ourselves to America. Fire-damp has exploded in the largest mine in the country, and I am sent to see the dead and the living brought up from the bowels of the earth. When this has been done the mine is declared closed until a blockaded shaft can be cleared out and a draught can be worked to clear the air and make it safe for men to work there. From pure bravado and folly I bribe a miner to take me down and through the gas-laden place. Though I did this, it is the sort of thing I wish to discourage, to condemn, to write against on all occasions. Whether in war or peace the correspondent who wilfully risks his life from a false sense of heroism degrades his business and violates his duty to the public and to his employer. However, I was young, and with another correspondent I paid ten dollars to be taken secretly through the mine. It did not occur to me that only a fool or a lunatic would help me in my folly, but I soon found it out. When we were in the heart of the mine the man began poking his naked lamp in the fissures and crannies above our head, saying: "Here's where the gas do be, and here, in such cracks like this." We had to use force to keep him from blowing up us and the mine, and to threaten him with violence unless he used the utmost discretion thereafter. After we were out of the great cavern and in the sunlight we thought with pleasure of the man's strange talk of the little brown folk who lived in the mine and appeared to warn the men when danger threatened —for he was a typical bred-in-the-bone child of superstition—a Welshman and a type.

On one night in the Kootenay country, Frederic Remington, the artist, and I had been fishing until after ten o'clock, enjoying the novel sensation of catching gamy and very large fish hours after most fishermen in other places imagine that fish have ceased to bite. At last we tired of the sport, and broke our way through the primitive and dense bush to the trail. Along that we toiled armed with nothing but our light fishing-rods. When we at last came to the shanty of some engineers whose guests we were, a man rushed up to us and asked if we had just come up the trail. We said we had. "Well," said he, "ten minutes ago I saw an immense puma going down the trail—the biggest I ever saw. How can it be possible you did not meet him?" There was only one explanation, of course—the puma was not hungry.

Across the border in the Canadian bush Remington and I were once upon a hunting-trip, with Cree Indians for our guides. One of these was the best hunter in the province, but a drunkard. We were warned of his besetting vice, and told that if he yielded to it while out with us our costly expedition would come to naught. On the first day, when we were miles from any habitation, I saw the Indian furtively stealing a bottle up to his mouth. Without reflecting, urged by my indignation, I snatched the bottle from his hand and flung it as far as I could into the forest. "You madman," said Remington, who was a hundred times more used to Indians than I; "he will brood over that until at last he will kill you, or try to. You must never do an angry thing to a savage unless you are prepared for worse from him." Therefore all that day our hands were ready to grip our revolvers and our eyes were on that Indian's every movement. Of course he said nothing; Indians seldom do. But nothing happened. The man forgot or forgave, or else was awed by our apparent indifference. It was my good-fortune that he was not a thoroughbred, pure-breed, wild red-man such as Remington shows by his stories and pictures that he knows as we all ought to know our Bible.

XI

The Power of a Reporter

THE editor of a great American newspaper once said, upon reducing the price of his newspaper to the public, that what he wanted was not money, but power. I cannot hold him up as an exemplar or guide in any phase of journalism, because he introduced yellow journalism to the country, and the corruption and demoralization of this part of the press began with him. Yellow journalism is but an episode, because its methods belong more naturally to the circus business than to our profession, and yet the love of power in a modern press-man is a development upon positive and actual conditions.

The modern journal wields great power—the greater the more shrewdly and broadly it is managed. And not only does every editor feel more or less of this possession of the means of influencing men and events, but his agents, the editorial writers and the correspondents, often see its effects even while they are producing them before their very eyes. The power of the editor of a newspaper of national importance is such that it can be exerted upon a government and upon the policy and laws of a people; but though the editor may feel the effect of his influence, he may be certain that it will never be publicly acknowledged. Vastly more direct and palpable is the far less public weight of a country or, as they say in England, a provincial editor. The effect of his counselling, his indignation, and his carefully considered verdict upon a matter of local interest is so instantly evident that one of the earliest dreams of most beginners in the profession is of owning a newspaper in a small town or city and thenceforth managing and directing his neighbors.

Those of us who never aspire to be more than "a big toad in a little puddle" cling to this ambition, and, in my opinion, happy men are they. They envy me and I return them the compliment, but I have "the best of the deal," because I have been a country journalist and know both lives. I once knew a country editor who was obeyed when he said "this bridge must be repaired," "that theatrical show must not be given here," "the gamblers who meet in such and such a place must be driven out of town," "this man must be elected and the other one defeated."

Without risking capital or limb or life, in the course of an easy, honorable, and dignified existence in which he enjoyed the leisure to become a scholar or whatsoe'er he pleased, this man ruled a community and ruled it for its good. Truly, I say, enviable is "the big toad in the little puddle."

In the course of the trial of Captain Dreyfus we had before us the proof of our power. You may say it was the unfinishable vitality of truth which reopened his case, but the French know very well that they had exiled truth and it found its opening in our foreign press. Except for the proof of our power they would have shut us out of the court-room; but though they hated us, and were frank to say so, they feared us to that degree that we were far better treated than similar critics and meddlers would have been treated in England or America.

The first "assignment" I ever had as a New York reporter was to go to Delaware to see a woman whipped. Half a dozen New York correspondents went to the jail in Newcastle on the day set for the whipping, and when we asked the sheriff to allow us to go in the jail-yard we told him plainly that if the woman was whipped we would be the means of arousing such indignation throughout the land that he would find no hole or corner in which to hide from the volcanic outburst of scorn and wrath that would pour down upon him. The sheriff brought out a travelling journeyman printer who, after sleeping in a railway coach, took away with him a coat which he found upon one of the seats. The sheriff intended to whip the printer with a dozen lashes, lightly, and he fastened him to the post and smiled as he thought how he would disappoint us and make us believe that a Delaware whipping was a trifling thing. But the printer did not fall into his plan. Humiliated, angry, and reckless, he waited for a perfect chance and then spat a mouthful of tobacco juice straight into the sheriff's eyes, momentarily blinding him. The sheriff, boiling with rage and smarting with pain, laid hold of the cat-o'-nine-tails, and, forgetting his earlier plan, wrapped the biting tails of the fearful instrument so fiercely around the printer's naked back that every stroke raised half a dozen welts and drew blood where the ends fell. Thus the woman—a poor creature who was sentenced for life—was saved from a whipping, for our disgust at what we had seen was so manifest that the sheriff did not dare to bring out the woman.

To descend to a little thing, as it will seem to my well-to-do readers, I once overturned an unjust law preventing the playing of barrel-organs in the streets of New York. I say I did it; in truth, I aroused the forces that did do it. I had too many thousand times seen what the playing of a street organ meant to the poor in the crowded tenement districts. I had seen how the children danced to its music, how their mothers came to the windows to lean out and listen, how the lads and the men drew near and whistled or sang to the tunes. I forgot how great a nuisance the same instrument was when I was trying to sleep, how such music jarred upon the educated tastes of us who can have true music when we want it. When the aldermen declared the street music forbidden I thought only of the million who loved it and who get far too little of pleasure. I wrote to all the newspapers, I interviewed their editors, I published letters, editorials, and descriptive accounts of what I had seen of the joyous and wholly good effect of these instruments in the world at our doors. The law was never put into effect, and soon afterwards it was annulled.

I have referred in a sentence to a question of veracity which once arose between a Secretary of State and myself. It was during the Chino-Japanese War. I happened to be in Shanghai when some Japanese students were arrested as spies and were locked up in the prison of the French Consulate. The United States had given its promise to protect all Japanese in China, and we were violating our pledge, because the minister who represented us in Peking had taken that moment of war as the time for enjoying his holidays at home and had left his son in his place. Japanese had been driven out of China without reason or proper notice, and now several were arrested and, as I well knew, were going to be tortured. Since no man may be punished in China unless he admits his guilt and asks to be punished, torture plays an important and necessary part in bringing about a pretence of compliance with this Confucian principle. Our consul-general gave me the fullest information in order to gain my aid, and was at the same time doing all he could to obtain the discharge of the prisoners. But as we had no men-of-war in Chinese waters the Chinese laughed at us in their sleeves. They took the Japanese from the French Consulate, hurried them to Nanking, and tortured them with horrible ingenuity and devilishness, every day with a new brutality, for seven days. Then they beheaded them. All this I knew to be true, but the Chinese minister at Washington told our Secretary of State that I was misinformed, and he believed the oily rogue and challenged my statements. Let no journalist ever forget the moral of what happened. Simply because I had never abused my opportunities by writing mere sensationalism, or untruths of any sort, the Senate took up the matter and, purely and solely upon my written word, as was there stated, it was turned over to the Committee on Foreign Relations for investigation and report. It ought not to have to be said—it is scandalous that there are newspapers and newspaper men who render such an admonition necessary—but the moral of this incident is that truth and right must ever be with the journalist who would do good in the world or who wishes to have influence and enjoy the use of it.

Once during the interval between two national political conventions I ran down into Southern Indiana to look over the region then terrorized by what were called the "white-caps." The country was fair to see—along the Ohio River it was an Eden—but scarcely anywhere had I seen such rascally, diseased, almost imbecile people. They were pure Anglo-Saxons, but were of the "poor white trash" order, and, having refused to allow foreigners or immigrants of any sort to share their land with them, they had gone on intermarrying and restricting their opportunities until mental and physical maladies abounded among them as if their country were an asylum for incurables. On no other great occasion have

I been alone, without the magnetic support of the influence of the press expressed by the presence of some, at least, of my colleagues. No one believed that I was a newspaper writer; the word flew like magic through the woods and the villages that I was a government detective. It had been expected that such a detective would be sent, and the shameful miscreants, who were practically all banded together and protected by the people, had vowed that if this detective attempted to arrest any one he should be shot. I travelled for several days in that land that seemed to groan beneath a curse. Here, in a leafy dell, I was shown where half a dozen men and women, returning from an open-air church among the trees, had been "ambushed" and fired into with shot-guns. There my driver showed me a house into which the "white-caps" had broken to take out two women and whip them because an unjust suspicion had tarnished their names. I was everywhere avoided as if I had the plague, and when I pursued my inquiries every one refused to speak, got out of my way, or lied to me. Above all else, I wanted to see the leader of the lawless woman-whipping organization, and at last, when I did not suspect that I was within miles of him, I was told that he was in the solitary shop or store of a village through which I was passing. The driver who was taking me from place to place dared not enter the shop with me. I went in by myself. I knew the ringleader from the descriptions I had heard, and when I entered the doorway I saw him turn his back as he stood among a semicircle of men. I walked straight ahead and put my hand on his shoulder. I was unarmed, and he was armed and surrounded by his bullies, yet he shrank under my touch and trembled like a leaf. I merely spoke his name, yet he let loose a torrent of denial and asseverations of his innocence and of my mistake in thinking him a "white-cap." I confess I could get little out of him except that he was never near where any outrages had occurred and that he knew I was a detective. But when I think how his guilt cowed him, and how, had he been a brave man, he could have set me to thinking of my own safety, I laugh at the recollection.

At the end of some days, when my head was strained with all that I had heard of the nocturnal operations of these scamps, I lay in bed in a hotel in that lawless region, fast asleep. Crash! crash! bang! went my door, and I sat bolt upright in bed, certain that I was the newest victim of the outlaws.

"Hang that door; it takes two men's strength

to open it," said some one. "It's all sprung out of shape. Here's your room, sir. I'll see if there's any water for you."

It was a false alarm. Another lodger had come for a night's rest, and a warped door had been forced to let him in. That is how most hair-breadth 'scapes turn out; that is the way with most of the dangers which our fancy builds up. The perils of even a correspondent's life are apt to be merely the "haunted houses" of his brain peopled with ghosts which prove to be mere wind or rats.

XII

THE VALUE OF HONESTY

THERE was a time in my newspaper career when it was hardly possible that any one supposed I should ever be competent to serve as a lamp to the feet of the humblest beginner. One of my own beginnings was in the position of local editor of the Tom's River *Courier*, a country weekly in New Jersey, to which paper I went with flattering recommendations. The editor, Thomas F. Joy, was deep and active in politics, and owned the only newspaper and printing-office in the place. I arrived on the night before election, and was left alone in the printing-office to get accustomed to my surroundings.

While I moved about the place, examining the machinery and type, a deputation of very respectable-looking citizens called and inquired for the proprietor. They knew that he had gone to bed to dream of his cleverness in having stifled all opposition to his political plans, knowing that his were the only ballots that had been printed, and that his circulars were the only arguments which were in circulation among his townspeople. Of all this I knew nothing, for I had not been three hours in the place. The shrewd men who called upon me had exactly taken my measure. They were sure that I would be anxious to do anything to distinguish myself on my first night in the town, and were equally certain that I could not see through their tricks. They told me what close friends they were with my employer, and urged me to repair some serious blunders which had been made in printing the election ballots. Eagerly I did my best to oblige them. I worked the whole night long. I set up a new ballot and printed thousands of copies of it. I set up a new circular and printed copies of that, also, by the thousand. Long after daybreak I went to my hotel, got my bath and coffee, and returned to the office of the *Courier*, proud of my industry. My pride was of short duration. The kindly editor of the preceding evening was now transformed into a very demon of ill-temper. He anathematized me as I never had been before and never have been since. He said I would never know enough to use an umbrella when it rained or to tell a gold coin from a bone button. I was not only dismissed forthwith, but I was almost blown out of his office by the tornado of his wrath.

The reason for this was explained when I mingled with the townspeople. Then I found that, ever so innocently, I had equipped the editor's opponents in politics with the means of completely defeating his plans. His rivals made a hero of me and proposed to establish me at the head of a newspaper of my own, but I was so humiliated over the way I had been duped that I would have none of their good-will.

My management of my first and only libel suit does not now seem to have been full of promise for one who would pose as an adept in the art of making a newspaper. I was then local editor of the *Standard*, in Red Bank, in the same State, a town in which there dwelt a noisy, tippling, scandal-mongering man whom all decent folk avoided. In a perfect state of civilization it would be impossible to slander or libel such a creature, who starts with no character, and can no more be damaged by truth or falsehood than you can hurt a bad egg by pointing at it with the finger of scorn. However, civilization was not (at that time) perfected in Red Bank, N. J., and when I published a few wholesome truths about this scamp he had the audacity to threaten to sue the *Standard* for damages. At this point the reader may need to be informed that the average editor dreads a libel suit beyond anything in the world. Some editors are suspected of looking under their beds every night for fear there may be a libel suit in hiding there. If all editors hated an untruth as they do a libel suit we should be basking in a journalistic millennium. I, who did not know all this, was simply astounded at the assurance of my victim in daring to pretend that he was libelled. One day, when I was in charge of the office, at the age of twenty, he clambered up the steep flight of stairs to see the editor. I told him I was acting for that dignitary. "You have treated me shamefully," said he. "Well, what more do you want?" I asked. "If you are not satisfied, there is plenty left to publish."

"I demand an apology," said he. At that I exclaimed: "Confound you, you old reprobate! Leave this instant or I'll throw you out of the window and—more than that—I'll thrash you every time I see you upon the street." "You shall sweat for this," said he. "You shall go bankrupt for this." Without another warning I lifted the man in my arms and threw him down the stairs. A hush fell upon the establishment. It would have fallen similarly upon the whole journalistic profession could all have known what I had done, for never was threat of a libel suit met in that fashion before. The editor came and behaved like a dead man, he was so frightened. As for my victim, the only thing he ever did was to get out of my way whenever he saw me out-of-doors during the next year or longer. Nevertheless, I do not recommend this method of meeting libel suits. The little boy who said that pins have saved thousands of lives merely "by not swallowing them" was right; in the same way libel suits have kept thousands of editors prosperous "by not having them."

I find I could easily provide material for half a dozen more chapters of this work; but there are two subjects in particular I should like to develop. One should be made up of incidents illustrating the value of absolute and incorruptible honesty in every writer for the press; the other should explain and exploit the value of what the first American college boys who went to England to row upon the Thames called "the get-there stroke." These two things—getting what we go for and keeping clean hands and open minds—are the surest elements of success in the craft.

At the Dreyfus trial I met a young man who lived in Paris as the correspondent of a London daily, and who told me that he secured his place by writing two pieces of news every day and sending them to that paper in London. During the first three months only three of his contributions were published. During the next three months very many were published. Then he asked for a salary, and it was given to him.

By his side there often sat, at Rennes, one of the oldest and most distinguished of English war correspondents. He had been sent, during the war between the United States and Spain, to describe affairs in Havana. Cuba was blockaded by American war-ships, but Mr. E. F. Knight, to whom I am referring, induced a ship captain to run the blockade and let him make his way ashore in a small boat. During the better part of two days that little boat was rolled upside down and rightside up in a tempest-lashed sea, and when at last he reached the shore he was at once thrown into prison as a spy. But he got there—to Havana, where he was sent. And he got there by the pertinacity which must have given him his first success and must continue to be his trump card so long as he plays this trying game. There is no resting on one's oars in this profession—no period of ease, no matter how well earned—no drowsy evening in the day of any correspondent's life. Mark that, whoever would enter the lists. Harbor no idle notion that you can win a different ending by special effort or ability. The harder you work the higher you may rise, but the higher you go the harder you must work.

Indomitable perseverance is not a quality upon which newspaper men hold an exclusive copyright, but it is one of the foremost requirements for preferment in our guild, and it is so much in evidence with us that I forget at times that any one may possess it, and I am freshly astonished each time that I see it employed in other walks of life. In the course of one of my journeys abroad I came upon an attaché of a United States minister whose duty it was to master the secrets of the military prominence of the country to which he had been sent. The dangerous and delicate expedients to which he resorted to get at these other people's secrets, the persistence, patience, and enthusiasm with which he conducted his work, the disregard he showed for his own comfort and convenience, make him a shining mark among men in my memory. I have known him to buy his way into a factory and to write with both hands, upon pieces of paper in his overcoat pockets, plans and notes of a piece of military machinery while pretending to be examining something else in another part of the room—some innocent apparatus like a pump or a turbine. And then I have known him to go home and work until broad daylight deciphering and elaborating the extraordinary notes he had made in his pockets. Secrecy like that is seldom necessary in the newspaper business, but such a "get-there stroke" would be sure to win a correspondent quick advancement.

I remember an amusing instance of my own "get-there" success. There had been a fire panic in a theatre, and this turned public attention to the question of the safety of the New York playhouses. We newspaper men knew that, though nearly all looked fair to the eye, most of the theatres were mere fire-traps, slenderly built, ill provided with exits, and so carelessly managed at the stage ends that nearly every one was, behind the scenes, a dangerous clutter of extra-inflammable material. When I set out to investigate the stage and dressing-rooms of every playhouse, admission was refused me at theatre after theatre. In spite of this, the work had to be done; therefore I went to an official of the Fire Department and induced him to obtain for me a suit of fireman's clothing and to constitute me an extra watchman at the theatres, with leave to watch in any and all of them. Every night I dressed myself up as a fireman and presented myself at the stage door of one of the theatres. I could not be shut out, and, as I aroused no suspicion that I was masquerading, no one tried to stop me. I enjoyed some famous talks with the leading American and English actors and actresses then playing in New York, during which they told me the most astounding facts about the shabby and dangerous quarters allotted to performers behind the scenes. Every day my reports appeared and puzzled and distressed the managers. But I did not begin writing them until I had visited more than half the theatres, and I never betrayed the manner in which I obtained the startling information which was thus conveyed to the public.

I suppose I could have obtained a hundred dollars from each of several theatres for glossing over the faults in their construction and management, but what a fool I should have been to take such money! Think of the plight of a man in a country possessing an honest press once he becomes suspected of "earning money at both ends of his work!" Note the worthlessness of the French press, which is almost altogether dishonest, the shabby standing of French journalists, their poor earnings, the precarious existence of most of the journals for which they write. I hear of critics at home whose houses are full of costly presents from those they have "puffed" and those they have spared. I hear of financial reporters who speculate on 'Change. I know of newspapers whose opinions and reading columns are open for purchase. Of all such I know that either ruin or lowered standing and greatly lessened profits are the result. The highest success and the greatest profits proceed, in the newspaper business, from serving the public single-heartedly, thoroughly, and with enthusiasm. Of all my work I am proudest of my service as a legislative reporter during two corrupt sessions of the Legislature of New York.

The editor of a Buffalo evening newspaper once wrote that four or five of us New York correspondents (Mr. Merlin, Mr. Spinney, Mr. Alvord or Mr. Hugh Hastings, and myself) had saved the people of the State many millions of dollars by simply disregarding our own opportunities for gain and protecting the public treasury against the scoundrels who tried to rob it. It is the literal truth, and, though I earned only seventy-five dollars a week and the excitement of exposing and angering the thieves, I never regretted the course I adopted. One of these light-fingered imitation statesmen was so kind as to offer me a thousand dollars down and a steady rain of heavy bribes if I would mend my ways. He truly said I might ride in my carriage if I would accept him as a counsellor and guide. But I knew a correspondent who was already in the pay of "the Black Horse Cavalry" (as we called the treasury raiders) and already rode in his carriage, and I knew that he was so despised of all men that, as I said, "I might take the money, but I should feel obliged to drown myself right afterwards for fear I might see myself in a looking-glass." The man who tried to corrupt me afterwards confessed that he was so afraid of God and his conscience that he dared not spend a night alone in bed, and therefore brought his little son to Albany to sleep with him. One day a combination of men was formed to remove me from my place, and a man of dignity and high position was sent to Mr. Charles A. Dana, my editor, to tell him that I was pursuing a mistaken policy and doing my newspaper a great deal of harm. "Yes, yes," said the great editor, "I suppose he does make mistakes, but we will keep him where he is because he is honest."

XIII

Election Night

MR. BENNETT showed his knowledge of the public curiosity when he put up a newspaper building so largely of glass as to reveal to the people in the streets the movements and something of the methods of the workmen who produce his daily journal. The crowds which gather at the windows betray the same interest in the subject that is shown wherever a reporter appears to do his work. To us who are engaged in the business, reporters seem all too numerous, and yet no sooner does one produce his book and pencil in a public hall or place than a whisper leaps from the mouths of the people, there is a visible stir to bring the man or woman into general view, and interest in the business in hand is thereafter divided with the newspaper historian. In some measure the newspaper directors have always made themselves responsible for that degree of mystery which clings to the business and keeps a keen edge upon the popular curiosity regarding it.

There are still newspaper editors who try to pose as petty czars before their subordinates, declining counsel and refusing explanation as a general in command would scarcely do in the heat of battle. There are newspaper establishments in which the editors' rooms are as difficult of access, even to the other workmen in the building, as an inventor's closet or the dressing-room of an actress; and there is not—and never can be—any newspaper office that is as open to the public as a store, or even as a bank. I once heard the editor-in-chief of a New York newspaper speak of "that mystery which the public always associates with the editorial sanctum." The utterance was priggish, but it sprang from a fact which has at its root the essence of journalism; for, if every one knew what was to be published in a newspaper, who wrote each article, and who furnished the facts, the business could not be carried on. What is meat to the mass of readers may be poison to the persons concerned, and, even as it is, there is a constant battle between those who are gathering the news and those who would like to keep it out of print.

Thus it is that, in maintaining some degree of mystery about the work, a great deal more comes to be fancied to exist, and the work of journalism remains greatly interesting to all—happily to those who live under its exciting influence as well as to those who get only occasional glimpses of its processes.

But there is one night in every year, in every great newspaper office, when work is done that is the least understood of all that goes on in the making of a daily paper; one night when the highest state of fever attends the excitement and strain of the most intense work that falls to the lot of any men, except soldiers in war. That is election night. That is the night when a few men sit down at six o'clock before virgin sheets of paper, with the knowledge that before two o'clock the next morning they must cover those sheets with the election returns of a nation, digesting mountains of figures and apprising the public of the results in the most condensed forms, weeks in advance of the official announcements, as sparks might be counted while they fly from the shapeless iron on a blacksmith's anvil. And these calculations must stand the test of comparison with those which the rival newspapers, working without collaboration, as eager competitors, will publish at the same moment. The mass of other news brings less responsibility and concern to the desk-men in such an office. It is guaranteed by great news associations, it is sent in by trusted correspondents from all over, everywhere. Each item or story is complete in itself. It needs only to be winnowed—the least interesting to be discarded, and the rest to be cut like cloth to fit the space at hand, and polished to suit the standards of the journal.

But the election figures come in driblets and atoms, and must be put together as the Florentines make their mosaics. Some of it, we shall see, is plucked from the very air—as a magician seems to collect coins in a borrowed hat—begotten of reasoning, but put down beside the genuine returns with equal confidence and almost equal accuracy. Ah! but that is a work to try cool heads and strong nerves. I am quite certain no other men in the world include such a night of tension and excitement, periodically, as a fixed part of a workaday existence. No other men, regularly once a year, feel themselves so truly in the focus of an intense public interest, manifesting itself in so many ways. If we could really put windows into our methods, as one of us has put them into his building, that, of all times and phases, would be the one whose illumination would cause the most surprise to the public.

The returns of every State are gathered by the leading newspapers in that State; and as there is a system of exchange between the newspapers, the chief care of each is to get the figures of its own

State. In New York City, then, the Empire State is the subject of most concern. It is an extraordinary State at all times, but never is it more so than when it is considered as a factor in a national election. It is not only one of the party battle-grounds—a pivotal, uncertain quantity—but it is full of big cities, rolling up enormous masses of votes; and at the same time it contains wilderness-districts, groups of counties covered by mountains and forests, where the railroads and telegraph circuits are few, and whence news leaks almost as slowly as from Montana or Idaho. To canvass it, to make ready to seize its returns on the instant, as if a giant hand were to be put out to cover every hill and valley, is the task of the managing editors—a task at once delicate and gigantic. Each managing editor has his own method, developed out of the traditions and resources of each establishment, and tested and strengthened year after year. The newspaper that is so economical as to rely on any press association, or even upon its regular correspondents, is not one that is valued for its election news. The journal that is so partisan as to arrange only for Republican or Democratic sources of information may be fortunate or may be wholly deceiving to its readers—as chance decrees. But the journals which are managed with pride in their correctness, in the getting and giving of the news regardless of even their own political leaning, such truly valuable journals take no chances, throw economy to the dogs, and yield to no bias in arranging to turn the floodgates of election news into their work-rooms on election night. A net is thrown over each county. The local political managers, the leading candidates, the correspondents in the country newspaper offices—all are ordered or requested to file the result of the voting as soon as they are known. Finally, personal friends of the editors and of the political writers are appealed to to "wire" the news as soon as it is determined, and special correspondents are detailed to wait upon the political chieftains and bosses, who are certain to be at their homes on that one night of the year, to send on the news that reaches them from their political agents. There are sixty counties in the State, and some are "covered" six or eight times in this way. Only fancy the number of telegrams that result from these arrangements, all superimposed upon the bales of despatches from the news associations! But the reader cannot conceive it. They rain in upon the workers like autumn leaves in a gale-swept forest. They cover the desks and the floor, and are piled in masses on the file-hooks before the night is over.

The services of the rival news associations and

of special reporters are engaged to hasten the gathering of the returns from New York City and the suburbs, in Staten Island, Long Island, New Jersey, and Westchester County, where the population is dense and where the election methods have always been more loose and dishonest than in the metropolis. Thus the State and parts of other States around it are picketed with nervous, active, earnest men, and thus the tension in the offices of the big dailies makes itself felt all over the State—and, by the same process, all over the Union. This same comprehensive surveillance operates strongly in producing and insuring a fair count. Time was—and not very long ago—when what are called the "back counties" were not under any such influence, and their returns were figured dilatorily, calmly, at ease—and often very dishonestly. Later far than Horace Greeley's time, when he demanded the best figures that were obtainable for his journal, there was far more tampering with the vote than even the most unprincipled scoundrels dare to attempt in these days. Only the other evening a politician told me something of this nefarious business, in which he used to be concerned, in a city not far from the capital of the State. The "bosses" who controlled the city used to have the returns read to them before the public had access to them. The "bosses" held back the additions in the heavily peopled wards where the voters of their party were most numerous. The returns they studied were therefore those of their antagonists. If these showed only a normal vote, they took no action, but if, as often happened, the ring rule had angered and stirred their opponents to poll a very heavy vote of protest, the bosses studied the vote, calculated its effect, and issued secret orders to their henchmen to "add a couple of hundred votes in the first ward," to "swell the vote in the third ward by five hundred," and so on, until, when they were ready to let the public have the returns, they were so doctored that the ring was seen to be still in power and the popular protest of no avail. To-day that cannot be done. In every district, at every headquarters, there is a company of reporters—impatient, resourceful, possessed of but a single aim, and confident in their knowledge of their rights as well as of their power—demanding the returns from this ward, from that one, from such a village—for the *Sun*, the *Times*, or the *Herald*, or the *Tribune*. "Colonizing" and "ballot-box stuffing" were reported to the newspapers from two places in New York State during the gathering of the revolutionary vote of November, 1893, but there were no returns held back to be doctored, and more than one "'boss" went down.

Now, to come back to one of the newspaper offices—to the one with which I am familiar and in which I have helped at this work year and year again—with such an annual dread of election night as to make it seem a state of millennium which those enjoy who merely read the papers after they are published. Imagine a great school-room in which there is no teacher's platform, with fifty or sixty desks facing all the cardinal points of the compass, so that each will get the nightlight and the daylight as best it can. Around the walls are the desks of the executive editors and of the copy-readers—the city desks, the suburban desk, the telegraph desks, the Washington and Albany desk, that of the night or "make-up" editor, and that of the managing editor. Within the hollow square fancy more than two-score reporters' desks, many of them pre-empted now for the election work, and these blanketed with great sheets of yellow blotting-paper, with fresh pads of writing-paper, with new pen-holders and pens *ad libitum*, with bristling rows of file-wires. The office is quiet and restful. The copy-readers are at their accustomed work of receiving and preparing the general, regular news. Of those who are to get up the election returns only two or three are busy early in the evening. They are those who are to receive the New York City returns, which begin to arrive by six o'clock.

The men who are to prepare the State table, by counties, the Congress table, and the legislative table of senators and assemblymen elected, are lolling in their chairs. Among them are men who are trained to the work and have been so trained because they have judgment, coolness, and the ability to work like lightning and with accuracy. The political correspondent, headquartered at Albany, has come to town with a complete general knowledge of the rivalries and conditions in each county. He has made up the legislative table in advance, prophesying the result of the election in each district as his judgment prompts him. He will be proud if he does not have to alter it in many places; but if there is an unexpected "tidal wave"—as our political revolutions are called—he will undo three-quarters of his work with an occasional grin that develops into a merry countenance as the night wears on, for your true journalist, who sees behind all doors and discovers the same chicanery and self-interest in all politicians, is very seldom a partisan. One man whom I know, and who knows us all, calls us all bashi-bazouks in politics, and in more or less other relations to life and citizenship.

Beside the "Albany man" sits the Washington correspondent—a nabob in the estimation of the staff, which grades the editor first, the managing editor second, the city editor third, the Washington correspondent fourth, and the London correspondent nebulously, with awe, as the pagans consider one of their gods that operate and yet are never seen. This Washington correspondent brings an unfamiliar, enviable atmosphere with him. Well-salaried, in command of a "bureau" and a staff of his own, he supports not only an elegance of attire, but an ease and a pride of bearing that are eloquent of a calmer atmosphere than the boiler-room energy of the home office. He has been heard of as smoking on the back porch of the White House with a President, and it is noticed that the editorial writers not only come out of the inner sanctum to gossip with him, but that they listen keenly and keep saying "Oho!" "Ah, indeed!" and "If that leaks out there'll be a stir." Possibly the chief of the special correspondents will be in this line of idle men—a diplomatic, easy-going man, who is a puzzle to the others because he eschews the executive desks that bring the modern high salaries to men as successful as he, because he has just come from South Carolina, and is going to New Orleans as soon as these figures are gathered

—a man who is perfectly at home in Paris, San Francisco, Quebec, and St. Augustine, and who has been heard to wish that he could make the acquaintance of his wife and children, since he has, he says, every reason to believe they are very nice people. There is more than one such "special," and if another of them is in town it may be that one who detests cities and civilization, who plunges into both wherever there is a war or an earthquake or a promise of rough adventure, only to return again to a little box he has built in a remote wilderness of mountains and woods, where he hibernates with wife and children, rod and gun, until the next call to danger.

But in the mean time the night grows. The managing editor has become the centre of the earliest excitement—if I may use a word that does not apply to any moment in newspaper life. Strain, tension, rush, busy-ness—these are all better terms, especially if taken together. The managing editor is the man who in reality "runs" a daily paper. He has charge of seven-eighths of an eight-page journal, of all but the editorial page and the forming and conduct of the journal's policy—a mysterious essence about which there is much nonsense and little that is productive of pecuniary profit in these days when the age demands that editors shall meet their readers with the same common-sense which the public now enjoys in quite as high a degree as themselves. An office-boy sits in the window behind the managing editor, and a stenographer has drawn a chair up beside that official's right elbow. The boxes that are shot out of a pneumatic tube leading from the headquarters of the principal telegraph company keep falling with a chug-chug, like the discharges of a musket—a startling, explosive noise that is to become incessant during the whole night. A bright office-boy—a sort of captain among these messengers — manipulates the tube. He opens the messages, and by means of a squad of other boys distributes them among the copy-readers and the men at work on the local returns. But all the news of the State, and of all the other States, he sends to the managing editor. That man is managing editor because he is calm and knowing and philosophical, because he is experienced, and because he understands how to manage men and a great newspaper without friction. How he does his work is marvellous. If the night editor tells him the printers are "getting drowned in copy," and that he cannot "get all the stuff in the paper," the managing editor simply clears his throat to get the general attention, remarks, "Keep the stuff down, boys; too much is going up," and then returns to his work in hand, well aware that not another word need be said.

In a moment of great pressure it may happen that an idle reporter tells a story that brings a knot of other idle men around him and evokes suppressed laughter. "Ahem!" says the managing editor, "too much noise here." After that every one hears the clock tick.

He is now the one who is drowned in "stuff." Scattered through the election despatches are requests for private news of the election from editors, candidates, governors of States, members of the cabinet at Washington, from school-boy friends up in the country, from great Wall Street operators and railroad magnates, from party "bosses" in several States, from all over and from all sorts of persons. "Can you say if I am elected?" "Give me the earliest tip you can on your State and city." "What do you hear from Ohio?" "We don't hear a sound from Virginia —what have you got?" These show the drift of hundreds of despatches. The managing editor reads the returns and hands them to the boy at his beck to distribute among the men at the desks. The private despatches he answers over his elbow to the stenographer.

Some one tells him that the crowd is forming in

front of the office. It is known as *the* crowd because it is always there on election night. It begins with a lot of little knots of men—one in front of the *Press*, another in front of the *Times*, the others in front of the buildings of the *Sun*, the *World*, the *Tribune*, and the rest. As these knots swell they join one another and blockade Park Row, and lap over into the City Hall Park —an enormous, patient, cheering, and yelling multitude of many thousands of persons, all with their white faces shining above their dark clothes.

"Tell —— to begin the bulletins," says the managing editor. Then he adds, "Tell the city editor to send me a bright reporter who can write bulletins all night." The bright reporter is found, and ordered to move about among the desks and learn "whatever will be interesting to feed to the crowd." The man who receives the order to begin the bulletins is the so-called "manager of the art department," a high-sounding title when one considers the pictures with which most newspapers entertain their readers—the best that rapid presswork permits, and yet none the better for that. This art manager does not intend to disappoint or thwart the crowd in front of his bulletin—for in front of each newspaper building a great transparency has been constructed. He spent the preceding day making portraits of well-known politicians and statesmen, as well as a great number of "comics"—hasty cartoons showing the Tammany Tiger on the deck of the battle-ship *New York*, showing Mr. McKinley triumphantly waving his tariff bill, as well as one showing the same gentleman buried under the same document, and one illustrative of a naval engagement in which the battle-ship *New York* is shelling the Tammany Tiger. He is a man of cheerful resignation and of resource—this art manager—and he prepares himself for what might be termed the Whatever. These pictures he draws in outline on small cards. Over each he lays a glass stereopticon slide and copies the drawing on the glass. Having dozens of these ready, he flashes one—a portrait—on the white canvas sheet. It is cheered. He follows it with "a comic." A roar of laughter follows. He cannot see the servile mob, and yet he manipulates it quite as if he should say, "Now I'll press a button and they'll howl," and "Now you shall hear them laugh." How like a newspaper man even this artist is—to remain unseen, unthought of, unknown, and yet to sway the crowd as he wills! The news bulletins begin to come later, and the words that compose them are painted on glass and magnified on the canvas, just like the pictures.

The first news, even from close at hand, is

always of one pattern. It consists of the returns of the brown-stone Republican districts, where there is only one vote or two to each house. It is easily counted, and so it is the first in hand. Along with it come calculations by the Press Association reporters—sent in on manifold sheets and reading like this: "48 *districts, official, give Republican vote of* 3,942; *Democrat*, 1,897; *same districts last year gave Republican*, 3,796; *Democratic*, 2,100." The chief one of the men who is taking the city returns is a born mathematician. He knows and loves figures, and handles them as Morphy played with chessmen. He employs ingenious, labor-saving, peculiar, and personal ways of dealing with them, and these blind despatches that rain in on him to the number of six hundred or seven hundred during the night he subjects to his logarithms and formulas with what looks like invulnerable patience, until—twenty times in the night—they tell him a growing and a widening story of ruin for one party and triumph for the other. At such times he seeks out each man engaged in similar work and says: "Did I tell you that Maynard was running behind the Democratic ticket? Well, he's running 10,000 behind." Later he made it 12,000, then 15,000, and at last about 20,000 behind.

In the mean time the office begins to fill with

people never seen there except on election nights, and with men who only come when great news is stirring. The latter were the New York correspondents of the great newspapers of the country, and of Canada and England. These were business-like. They whispered to the managing editor. They wanted figures, they wanted proof-sheets, they wanted the editorial utterance of the paper that was to appear next morning, and they wanted reasons for the turn the voting was taking in Brooklyn and Buffalo, where the people overturned the governments. Others were the editorial writers, among them those who only work in the daytime and those who never come to the office at all, but send their essays in by mail and messenger. They know little of the methods of any department of a newspaper except their own, and the fact was betrayed in their uneasiness, their surprised look when they saw the main work-room brilliant, lighted as the streets at noon—and crowded—with a hush upon it that they did not expect, suppressing their after-dinner tendency to talk. They noticed, too, that the office-boys vouchsafed them no deference, but elbowed them out of the way. And when they essayed to joke with the Washington correspondent and the Albany man, one of those gentlemen said "Yes—yes; but I am busy; excuse me." With the editorial writers had come some notable public men found at the clubs and eager to come down and get the news—a federal senator, a bibulous Western editor, a judge or two, and a general of the regular army. There is no reverence among newspaper men. They know humanity too well not to see beneath the mere uniforms and robes by which men are told apart. So, presently, these gentlemen withdrew to the sanctums where the art manager and his assistants bustled to and fro among them in order to display the bulletins out of the windows. But the notables endured the discomfort, while one of the editors went to and fro, getting outlines of the exciting election from the managing editor.

The publisher came up from the counting-room—a man of affairs and the personage who grows more and more important as the capital involved in newspaper work swells and keeps swelling—withal, a practical man who read the situation as a telegrapher reads the Morse alphabet. He came merely to ask if anything was wanted. Yet but for the fact that everybody else was there, it would have seemed strange to see him downtown after dark. The racing reporter came in, drawing off his red gloves and his sleek beaver coat. An enthusiast, he had much to tell of the day's events at some great race-course, but no one would listen; in fact, he became the listener to news that even he recognized as more important than his own. After getting all that was then known of the trend of the voting, he—upon whom the news had thus been forced—remarked: "If that is all true, I win eight hundred, two hats, and an overcoat." Then he sat down and wrote the report of the races about which no one seemed to care.

There sauntered in, presently, a short, ruddy-faced, foreign-looking man of the Slav type of features—such a man as those you see by the score in the polyglot crowds at the East Side cafés and reading-rooms. He neither looked at nor spoke to any one, but, taking an apple out of one pocket and a Buda-Pesth daily out of the other, began to read print that appeared to be upside down. He was the chess editor. The bustle of the office surged around him without touching him at any point, until a boy brought him a yellow telegram. He dropped his newspaper, read a line, put down his apple, put on his glasses, and became a new man, totally unlike the stolid Hungarian who had been in his clothing a moment before. What he read was something like this:

"ST. PETERSBURG, *November 7th.*

"Wishnakief Arnald 48, 19 centre gambit 11, 36, 49, 12, Queen 16 Knight and Bishop. Excitement. To-morrow end."

Yet his eyes distended, he slapped his knee with his free hand, he ran to a cupboard and took out a chess-board, and, after twenty minutes spent in studying some moves that he made with his chessmen, he sat down, and in a fever of excitement tossed off a dozen pages of a report of a spirited episode and some startling new modes of play in a game of chess in Russia.

In the mean time the pneumatic tube kept up its explosions, the leather cups stuffed with telegrams came like bullets from a rapid-fire gun, and the men at work on the election figures were as busy as bees. While each man worked his way through a great pile of despatches kept under one hand, the boys threw other telegrams in front of him, until half his mind was occupied in keeping those he had not looked at from becoming mixed in with those he had used. Light was coming out of the confusion of telegrams. The mosaic was beginning to reveal its pattern. Ohio had gone Republican. So had Brooklyn and Buffalo. There was unexpected news from Virginia and Illinois. The pattern was distinct, but scores of little cubes were missing. The figures did not come from Erie, St. Lawrence, Rockland, Yates, and other counties. There was doubt as to the senatorial election in the Dutchess district, and about a senate district in Kings. The howls and cheers of the multitude in the streets were growing tiresome. It was disquieting to know that the crowds in front of the *Tribune* and the *Times* were cheering something when there was no time or way to find out what that something was. It was tiresome, too, to have one's mind distracted when the climax of the work was approaching. The despatches were coming to fill up the missing details, but the worst of it was that the clock hands were moving much faster. Presently the managing editor would be certain to walk round the desks, to hear how each table was progressing, and then to say, quite regardless of all the omissions and uncertainties: "Well, I'll give you all twenty minutes; everything must be closed up in twenty minutes, the tables footed, and the stuff up-stairs."

That order had not come, to be sure, yet it certainly was at hand, and it would never do to think of it, for to lose one's coolness would be to delay and even to "'bungle" the newspaper which most prides itself on its election returns. And yet all was still confusion, and two dozen important counties and contests were either unheard from or left in a muddle of doubt. To clear up these points as many telegrams had been hurried off, and office-boys stood in a little queue awaiting their turns at the long-distance telephone that was in use to prod up men in Connecticut, in Syracuse, on the edge of the Catskills, and at the far end of Long Island.

The chief leader-writer had been hidden in an inner room writing the editorial comment on the night's news. He had thought of a sub-editorial paragraph that greatly amused him. He showed it to one of the busiest men at the election desks, a man on whose brow a cold sweat had already formed in anticipation of the rush and worry of the approaching climax. Still, a chief leader-writer always commands deference and polite attention. The unfortunate calculator took the editorial manuscript and looked at it. To the man in the next chair the handwriting appeared to be Greeleyesque, illegible, fly-trackish.

"I rather like that," said the leader-writer.

"Yes, it's very good," said the man of figures.

"I think I'll let it go," said the editor.

"I certainly should," said the other.

When the leader-writer had gone some one asked the other man what the editorial was about.

"It looked like what is carved on the obelisk in Central Park; I could not read a word of it," said the man of cold sweat, "but I had no time to tell him so."

From some counties the official figures have

come in—perhaps from more than half—and more are coming every minute. But from others there are six, and even eight, different, contradictory returns—running the majorities up and down a width of a thousand votes apart. The man who knows how each county is in the habit of voting, and how half the other counties have already voted, must fix upon one of these figures and adopt it in his table. Thus he must, at the last moment, run through the entire list. The managing editor comes, as was foreseen, but he shortens the time. "Have all the tables footed and up-stairs in fifteen minutes, and each of you must write a short introductory story explaining whatever is extraordinary and peculiar in the situation. I want a paragraph, also, from each of you, for the main introduction that is to lead the paper."

Is he insane? Well, if he is, there is no time to try to cure him now. "Yes, sir; it does not seem possible to do all that—but we'll do it." Then comes the ecstasy of that night's whirl—a sort of controlled delirium in which the mind is held down to its work by some unaccountable extra agency which may be a part of itself, and yet which operates against and over itself. The figure spaces are filled in—each set of numerals being studied, selected, and set down, each in the bare moment of poising a pencil. If there aren't any figures to choose from (indicating the vote of some county in the Adirondacks or of some farming county on the Pennsylvania border), one must recollect what such counties always have done and must imagine how they would feel the same influences that have altered the accustomed vote elsewhere all over the State. Down go the missing figures, grasped out of the air, and presently the table is ready to foot up. So are the other tables over which all the men are straining. The riot of noise in the street below is growing less and less. The bulletins have exhausted the news and the people are going home—visibly melting away. The office clock begins to tick again. The hush in the office is painful. As each table is footed it is exchanged for another, and the calculators go over and verify one another's figures. "I can't make this one come out as you did," says one. "Well, you must," says the other; "it came that way twice over, and it must be right." Then a moment's pause, and, "It is right; who said it wasn't? Here, boy, send this up." The composing-room, where the manuscripts are turned into type, is never spoken of except as "up" and "up-stairs."

Thus the tables are hurried out of the way. But the pneumatic tube continues its chug-chug, and the boys keep shelling the leather cups and pouring the telegrams upon the desks—to be used in a second edition, for which all the work is soon to be gone over again.

"Hurry up your introductory matter," the managing editor says, with a calmness and amiability that are maddening. "You have still six minutes."

After all, when every man's head is full of his work and the tension is still drawn, it is not difficult to do a little more. What is a fourth hand-spring to a man who has already turned three? Besides, a newspaper man's capability is like a street-car—"there is always room for one more." And a few lines set in large type and "leaded" will look twice as long as ordinary matter.

Even while these thoughts are flashing through their minds, one man is describing the complexion and changes in the State legislature, with side-lights on the queer turns of fate that overtook men here and there in various assembly and senatorial districts. Another is explaining the results of the righteous defeat of the "ring" in Buffalo, the failure of Albany and Troy to respond to sentiments and influences that shook all the other cities and counties in New York. Another is sweeping his mind's eye all over the Union, and telling what went on in every State, at all the polls. Boys are seizing the wet sheets and flinging them into the iron basket that travels up and down inside the wall of the building, to and from the crowded work-room of the lightning-like compositors, with its alternate rows of shadows and electric beams. At last — at ten minutes to two o'clock, the great daily paper is all written.

Hot coffee is brought up from a near-by restaurant, bottles of beer are being opened with a pop and a splash, grapes and sandwiches are being devoured by men who are all on their legs, relieving the strain of long sitting. In what seems less than five minutes, quickly as the same delirious speed of the printers and pressmen can accomplish it, the paper itself, damp and ready to smear wherever it is touched, will be on the managing editor's desk with all the chief men of the office gathered behind the managing editor, looking at it over his shoulders. And, even as they look, a boy will throw over their heads the *Herald*, just as wet and fresh. And then the next, and the next, and the next of the dailies will arrive—until all the morning papers are there. Each is compared with the one gotten out by ourselves. No two agree exactly, though all are in the main alike; but it is observed that the winning party is credited with a larger majority in our journal than in any of the others.

"How do you account for that—are we all right?" the managing editor inquires of the man who figured that majority.

"Dead right," says the man addressed; "we'll have to put it higher yet in the second edition."

A moment later a whisper runs from mouth to mouth, and twenty heads are turned towards a bearded man who is calmly writing at one of the desks, utterly heedless of the general curiosity to see the rival journals, oblivious of all the excitement over the elections, at peace amid all the strain and wear and tear of that night of nights.

"He's been in Africa since eight o'clock," one editor whispers. "He does not know there has been an election."

"Who is he?" asks one of the "specials."

"He is the geographical editor. I'll bet a dollar he is in Australia or Patagonia—let's look and see."

The man who last spoke walks over to a point from which he can read what the placid editor is writing. This is what he reads:

"The Maxim guns proved more than Lo Bengula could meet. Bulawayo, his capital, was not fortified for modern warfare. It is a small—"

"Now, then, gentlemen," says the managing editor, "let's cut the tables out of the first edition, paste them on good big sheets, and go to work again. The despatches that have come in while we have been loafing will supply whatever we missed, and if we don't come close to being absolutely correct I miss my guess. Now, then, let's rattle up the second edition."

XIV

The Special Correspondent

A VERY intelligent man read with much interest the project of M. de Blowitz for manufacturing newspaper correspondents, and it is fair to presume that some were impressed by it. I do not agree with him—not even with his preliminary assumption that journalists can be made at all, except as (when the world shall advance to the point the Mormons aim at) we shall arrange for all sorts of human talent, as we now do for various points of excellence in horses and milch-cows. Professor Brainard G. Smith, of Cornell, knew that, even when he presided over the class or school of journalism at that university. He was criticised and ridiculed by a hasty and ignorant number of journalists, who supposed that he aimed to establish a factory for turning out newspaper men as sashes and blinds are produced. He never was nonsensical. He aimed only to teach composition, as the now lost art of letter-writing was taught one hundred years ago, by precept and example. He offered to take those who thought they wanted to be newspaper men (I like that honest, modern word better than the word journalist), and to give them a chance to write articles as for a newspaper, while he talked to them about the work, supplied them with examples of what was best in the ways of reporting, and "edited" their "copy" as he had done on a daily newspaper in days gone by. The only question was whether such a department ought to be included in the plan of a college—or even in that of a technical school—since the fellows who have the gift would still have to begin at the bottom when they took up regular work, and would best learn the little that can be taught about newspaper writing when they were set to acquire the knowledge by such degrees as would regulate their ability to earn much or little at the business.

Newspaper men are born and not made. I do not mean that the art of contributing skill in modern newswriting or editorial work is any nearer to heavenly standards than the reader holds it to be, whatever his opinions are; but the phrase "heaven-born" expresses what it is. It cannot be taught or manufactured in a boy. There are persons in northern New York who are hoarding the scraps of paper whereon my friend Frederic

Remington scrawled the childish drawings by means of which he gave hint of what his life-work was to be, and it is such an essence as he possessed which must be in the journalist in childhood. The peculiar faculties of a blacksmith are in the prospective blacksmith in the same way, and others are in the future money-maker, the future architect, and the future horse-doctor, if you please, as well. The man who is or is not a born newspaper man either can write entertainingly and with some sense of color and proportion about the things that are interesting or important—or he cannot. If he can, that ability must be developed and fashioned, not according to any so-called "tricks of the trade," however, for the artist or preacher or doctor or writer who follows only the cut-and-dried rules of his calling is a mere bush that does not flower. If he does not develop his own methods and "style," he will never amount to much beyond getting his living.

There are newspaper editors, as there are "art directors" and college professors, who think this is all humbug. They are like the old English fathers who put the first son in the army, the second one in the navy, and the third in the church. Such men do not recognize the quality called "genius," except where it is so pronounced as to be overmastering. The father of the elder

Charles Mathews distinguished his kind when he set out to follow his son and hiss him off the stage, but desisted on the first night because the boy made him laugh so that he could not hiss. Such are the stubborn folk who now and then pop up in newspaper offices, and establish business rules and talk of "discipline," who suspend and fine and lecture the writers who are under them. It does not do, and there lies a proof of the old-fashioned idea that talent is innate and not manufacturable. The self-effacement of a newspaper correspondent is not that of a soldier; it is that of a scout. These martinets can decimate their forces, they can weed out the talent and hold fast to the sticks, and they can crush down *esprit de corps* and greatly weaken a newspaper; that is all. Newspaper making is not a business, except in the publication office. It is not a business—as the word is meant to be used—in the editorial or reporters' rooms. The kind of brains that are powerful there would not fit a man to earn his salt in trade.

How can any one hope to succeed while fettering with business rules such enthusiasm, perseverance, self-sacrifice, courage, ingenuity, wit, cheerfulness, and tact as go to make up the successful modern reporter of the first or second grades? The average worker for wages begins a fixed routine at a certain hour every day, performs it, and goes back to his home and his own pleasures in eight or ten hours; but this queer creation of the period, the newspaper man, penetrates the wilds of Athabasca in midwinter to find a white girl who is said to be in the custody of Indians; floats about in the bay or ocean for days to meet a steamship; sees himself locked and battened in an untried submarine boat, as Stephen Bonsal did not long ago, to be shot down to the bottom of the harbor in that perambulating coffin; or at a moment's notice goes to Hamburg when it is the hotbed of a cholera epidemic, to put up there and report what he sees. This singular creature can make no appointment with wife or friend, even a day in advance. He cannot predict where he will be living next year or next month. He is not surprised, on coming back from a wearisome journey at midnight, to find that he is ordered to start on another expedition in five hours. He does not deal with his own kind or any special sort of men, but with all kinds, under all circumstances; and having written an account of a week's stay aboard the most luxurious steam-yacht of the period, he goes post-haste to witness a miners' riot in the mountains of North Carolina. All that is *a* business, if you please, but it is not what men call "business." A newspaper is a co-operative concern in all except an equal division of the earnings; and since a good half of the newspapers do not more than pay their way, it is good for the writers that the co-operative tendency stops where it does. The more thoroughly a newspaper manager relies upon the enthusiasm and pride of his men, the more considerable is his success. The office of the only newspaper I know well—the *Sun*—which most journalists regard as the most brilliant and most wide-awake product of their profession, is frequently likened to a club-house. No taint of caste poisons its atmosphere or forces its workers into cliques, and when its men have no work to do they play together, at cards or chess or gymnastics, or whatever.

No newspaper has gone so far in pressing the practical view of the character of newspaper enterprises as the *Evening Post*, which calls our newspapers speculative concerns that gather news to sell it at a profit. This is the business idea which, as I say, is correct, in so far as the publication office is concerned. Yet it cannot have been a mere clerk who gathered the data for that journal's biographies of the machine politicians of New York; nor was it an accountant or salesman who commented upon these records in the editorial columns, for clerks do not perform that sort of work, nor do wages alone pay for them.

The *Evening Post* is one of the very ablest and best newspapers in America, and its practical view of the profession of which it is a product must be regarded as one among the many eccentricities that give it distinction, even when they do not add to its worth.

What I have said of journalism is part of that which applies to the subject in hand—the special correspondent, or, as they call him in England, "the special." The mere reporter who always remains a reporter, with a department to cover or errands to run, may or may not be especially gifted. The special correspondent must be "to the manner born." He may or may not have creative ability. That is essential to the sketch-writer, whether he does his work on the editorial page or supplies the character sketches that make too little renown for the men who write beside the news-columns. But the special correspondent must have a great many other qualities of an uncommon kind, and in a remarkable degree. He must have such a temperament as to be new-born every morning, and to look on all that he is to write about with new eyes and fresh interest. He must have a made-to-order sort of a soul, that will suffer itself to be thrown into whatever he does as a boy's soul enters into what games he plays at college. He must have at once the broadest and the finest power of observation, and the vocabulary and facility that are the bases of expression and freedom with his pen. He must be as sanguine as a song-bird, and as strong and willing as a race-horse. Above all, he must love his work better than his comfort, his club, his home, or his friends, else he might some day pause and consider for what small reward and shadowy glory he is risking his neck or plunging into discomfort—a train of thoughts which can never come to a correspondent as it does to men of many another stamp who live for money, for comfort, or for social distinction. He must have a personality all vigor to keep on past every hinderance, and with much candor and sweetness to win and keep men's confidence, so that they will admit him everywhere and talk to him unrestrainedly; but his personality must be of a kind that does not intrude itself too rigidly at many points, for, like an actor, he must be controlled by some other's character and appetite and likes—those of the public. If he consults his own whims or feelings, or has stiff prejudices of his own, they must be very strong indeed—so strong as to subordinate both the public and his newspaper to his individuality. And then, in my opinion, he will be one of several forcible and eccentric writers whom we could all name, but he will not be the ideal or the typical special correspondent. Such a man will be apt to twist his facts to make them accord with his wishes, and in this case, if I employed him, I would send another and a genuine correspondent to make separate reports of the same matter, that my readers who liked the strong man's crotchets could have them, while all the readers could get the news as well.

The special correspondent must be so constituted as to remain poor, and willingly, so long as he sticks to newspaper work. There have to be such men in a world that is as well ordered and complete as this—who write about what may make or ruin fortunes, and yet feel only a chronicler's interest in getting at the truth concerning them. I will not say what would happen if their palms itched, because they next to never do itch. Such is the peculiarity of their minds that, without the feeling of pariahs or the impulses of Bedouins, they consider nothing but their duty to the public. They want neither credit nor sympathy. It is their nature. In spite of the speculative character of a newspaper enterprise, it is to the public that the newspaper correspondent appeals one hundred times for every time that he is even asked to consider the whims or interests of the men who own the paper. If there are editors or owners who are not nearly equally disinterested in the collection and publication of the news, they are fools, and must be content with less than the fortune with which the public is certain to reward those who are.

There was once an idea that such men as the true "specials"—content to do superhuman and dangerous work for a salary and expenses—were apt to end in becoming a charge on their friends or the public, and were not to be wondered at if they were drunkards. A great many erratic, irresponsible geniuses and mock-geniuses, from the days of the *Spectator*, in all likelihood, down to those of Pfaff's beer cellar, not long ago, were borne with and even encouraged under that notion. It was a wrong one. The special correspondent is trained to be a great expense to himself, because, when on duty away from home, he must live so as to acquire expensive tastes; but the day has gone by when either his employers or associates will put up with any form of unreliability or blameworthiness in his habits or his principles. The need of a barber and a bath, and the tenancy of an attic with a bottle in lieu of other furniture, are no longer recognized as the outward proof of even poetic ability.

The correspondents of to-day must be and are welcome at the houses, clubs, and business places of the men who lead in public affairs. They must be men of parts and of good appearance and behavior. This is the day when a woman has interviewed the Pope, and a reporter has been nominated for mayor of Brooklyn (failing in which effort he became the model postmaster of the country). Nothing about the profession is more remarkable than the change that has come over the relationship between the correspondent and the so-called "great man." While there are reporters who "hound" public men, there are also public men who badger the newspaper folk. The typical correspondents, on the other hand, call upon the officials upon terms of equality and get from them what they want—to publish or not to publish, as the two agree. The best Washington correspondents work upon a friendly basis with cabinet officers and senators—all of them that they care to know—and are recognized as men pursuing an honorable calling. I once congratulated an English reporter, who told me he had reported Gladstone's speeches for nearly twenty years, upon knowing that statesman so well. "God bless you," said he, "I don't know him at all. I was once unable to escape from his car without passing him, when he came in unexpectedly, and a mutual friend introduced me to him. But I never presumed upon that, you know." Such a man and many others in England have wondered at the place the best American newspaper correspondents have managed to carve out for themselves by earning the confidence and friendly interest of public men.

Two things the critic of the modern newspaper man is very apt to overlook. One is that nine times in ten, when a man's affairs become of interest to the public, he is as anxious to see the newspaper man as the other is to see him. The other thing is that a shrewd man, who recognizes the place the press has taken and the power it has, will easily manage to make it serve him to some extent while he is serving it. It serves him gladly if what he wants is of value or of interest to the public. A noble personage was once asked by an American what he could say to the reporters at home about something that concerned them both, and which had been discussed in this country by means of the cable.

"Tell the reporters to go to the devil," said the exalted foreigner.

"Oh, but I can't," said the American. "Our American way is to help each other along. I like to read about other men in our papers, and I must contribute my share to the fund of news. I will have to tell them whatever will do no harm for the public to know."

That illustrates another element in the situation that is helpful to the modern correspondent, and if he did not take full advantage of it, what a poor workman he would be!

The element of danger sometimes plays a part in the adventures of a man whose life is spent in minding the business of others, on behalf of the rest of mankind; but a peculiarity and a charm of that life is in the fact that he can never tell when or where the danger will arise. I have found it the next thing to a certainty that when the most unsafety is looked for the least is found, whereas when none is expected it often springs to the foreground. At the risk of repeating myself I will illustrate this with the following incident. Being sent into southern Indiana to investigate the Whitecaps, not long ago, I anticipated great mischief from the low-lived cowards who are so numerous in that region, and who compose the meanest lot of human beings I ever saw — the meanest in morals, the poorest in substance, the most frequently diseased and deformed in body. They are a people run to seed by means of an exclusiveness that has limited a host of them to a few surnames, and that has shut out new population at the point of a gun, the gun being always fired at the back of its victim. There had been reason enough for going there in reports of many cowardly and brutal outrages, but the truth, as I found it, was that the state of affairs was ten times worse than it had been reported. The night riders were out in almost every village, masked and armed, and bent on whipping women as often as men. Every here and there the scenes of murders and outrages were pointed out. Even a little gully-road leading to the principal out-door religious meeting-place of one county had been the scène of a fight wherein men in ambush shot others who were on their way home from church on a Sunday night. Just as I reached that region a rumor had gone forth that the Federal government meant to send a Secret Service or Pinkerton man to spy out every leader in every outrage that had taken place. It was commonly agreed that I was that official. I did not know it at the time, but even the law-abiding folk in the towns along the Ohio River discredited my assertion that I was a newspaper man, and spread the belief that I was a detective. There was one especially bad nest of Whitecaps that it was necessary to go to in order to talk to the perpetrators of a long list of midnight outrages. I reached the place and found the leader—the terror of the country-side—loafing in a cross-roads store with a friend or two, and several others who held the middle course—quite popular in such a time and place—of being mortally afraid of, and excessively polite to, the Whitecaps.

The chief rapscallion, whom I wished to interview, seemed to me at the first glance to be seven feet high and as rawboned and vicious-looking as a wolf. He tried to keep his back towards the open floor-space in the store. My visit was expected. All had gathered there when it was known that I had come to the town. I asked a few pointed questions of the store-keeper, and got some exceptionally dull answers. Then I inquired for the ringleader. No one pointed him out or answered me. All the men looked at the floor. I never was more certain that I was in for a lot of trouble. Having the man's description well in mind, I advanced and touched his arm lightly with my fingers. It was like touching a mould of jelly. He quivered all over. All my anx ety vanished at once. The man was a cur, and his fright was almost pitiable to witness.

"Colonel, I don't know nothin' about that scrape at ——'s," he said; "I kin prove I was ter hum all that night—and all the other nights—and hain't had nothin' to do with no Whitecap business"—all this before I had accused him of anything whatever.

He supposed himself in the toils of a detective

of dime-novel caliber, from whom nothing could be hidden, and only capital punishment could be expected. He was by nature as harmless as a turtle-dove to any man in the daytime. It was at night, with his rawhide swung over a woman's naked back, that he played his dangerous part.

I have been asked to write upon this subject of the newspaper correspondent, and to illustrate what I write with my own experiences. It will be an easier task—and pleasanter for the reader—if it is understood that, while describing the qualities of the perfect and typical man of this sort, I am not thinking of myself. As a correspondent I have only been what I have been. What I would like to have been is the kind of man who is here described.

If I have done anything uncommon in newspaper work, it has been in the way of reporting the main stem of important events completely, and at great lengths, unaided and alone. It is said that in New York, at least, I have been peculiar in possessing the—physique is perhaps the greatest requisite—to carry out tasks of the sort, necessitating the nearest approach to an imitation of ubiquitousness, and resulting in from seven to ten columns of solid writing for the next day's paper. Some curiosity as to how this is done has been manifested by others in the profession, and I have been asked to explain it, but it seems to me there is little to tell. Take for an illustration the last inauguration of a President. I had myself called at five o'clock in the morning, and having a cab at hand, mounted the box with the negro driver and travelled about the city from end to end and side to side. I did this to see the people get up and the trains roll in and the soldiers turn out — to catch the capital robing like a bride for her wedding. After a breakfast, eaten calmly, I made another tour of the town and then began to approach the subject more closely, calling at the White House, mingling with the crowds in the principal hotels, moving between the Senate and the House of Representatives, to report the hurly-burly of the closing moments of a dying administration. I saw the old and the new President, and then witnessed the inauguration ceremonies and the parade. Then, having seen the new family in place in the White House, I took a hearty luncheon and sat down at half-past one o'clock to write steadily for twelve hours, with plenty of pencils and pads and messenger-boys at hand, and with my note-book supplemented by clippings from all the afternoon papers (covering details to which I might or might not wish to refer). Cigars, a sandwich or two at supper-time, and a stout horn of brandy late at night were my other equipments.

That is hard work, but it is as nothing, in that respect, when compared with the task of reporting a national convention in the same way. One needs only to *see* an inauguration; in a national convention one must *know*. The leading men, their records, motives, and plottings, must be known. If one such man is absent from the convention-hall, it must be known where he is and what he is doing. There is nothing in all the business that compares with a national convention for trying the body and mind of a man who essays to master and report it; that is, if he works for a newspaper which wants the truth, regardless of its predictions or policy. In the course of it there comes a task beside which the rest of it has been trifling. That is, the "covering" of a night session when the balloting is in progress.

Then the reporter of the main story selects the ablest man on his staff and asks him to stand beside him and whisper everything that he sees. The reporter is seeing for himself, but must write as well, and so may miss a word or a tableau. He is writing as for his life. He has a man to keep sharpening his pencils and to hand his copy to the telegraph-boys, who are throwing themselves at him and away from him like balls out of cannon. Sometimes he is allowed to finish twenty words on a sheet, but more often the pages are torn from under his pencil with only eight or ten words on each one. His desk is a board; men are clambering over him, the place is in a tumult. But all that and the strain conduce to good work. The strain! He knows that the hungry maw of the printing-press in New York is wide-open, that the wires are loaded, that his matter is being seized and flung into extra editions, and that all around him are men as able as himself, doing the same work, and determined to excel him at it if they can. The fevered pencil flies, every nerve is strained, every brain-cell is clear. Comment, description, reminiscence, dialogue, and explanation flow upon the impatient sheets in short paragraphs, like slivers of crystal. There is no turning back, no chance for correction or rearrangement, no possibility of changing a word that has been written. Yet there must be no mistakes, no confusion or complexity. For two or three hours, perhaps even longer, this race is kept up. That is the hardest task that falls to the lot of a "special," and it is the most intoxicating. Whoever does it is glad that he has lived to drink so deep a draught of that matchless elixir which keeps us all young till we die—excitement.

To "beat" his fellows is still the chief aim and glory of every man who writes on the newspages, but the "beat" (as an exclusive piece of news is called) is growing to be more and more a product of intimate acquaintance with public men, and less and less a result of agility of mind and body. The great press associations now scatter the news of important happenings indiscriminately, and special correspondents do very little racing with locomotives and tugs, and still less telegraphing of the Bible — a favorite trick of a bygone day, accomplished by instructing a telegraph operator to send off your "copy" and then supplement it with the book of Job or Revelation so as to busy the wire until it was too late for any other correspondent to send in his news. The last time I tried that my competitor rowed across Haverstraw Bay in a storm, and, from another point, sent in a story as complete as my own. The old-fashioned competitions now occur in lonely country regions, where the facilities for telegraphing are so meagre as to tempt a man to try to control them. I remember a delightful half-hour when a *Tribune* man tried to reach a country wire first in order to shut me out. We had to run three miles over a plain that was one great glare of ice. He was the faster runner and appeared to have everything his own way, but suddenly he slipped and rolled down the side of a gully to fetch up at the bottom badly hurt. The tearing of his clothes and peeling of his face did not bother him, but his ankle was sprained and he could not walk without help.

"I give up," said he. "Will you help me to the village?"

"I don't know," I replied. "Is the wire mine?"

"Of course," said he; "I'm done." But I gave him his turn at it. The matter did not warrant shutting him out.

Constituted as I am, the comic side of my own experiences has always interested me greatly and filled a large place in my memory. Of one long ride in the wilderness beside Lake Superior, for instance, I recall, first, the splendid beauties of the woods, and, next, the comic habit of my French-Canadian guide in always speaking of the Indians of the neighborhood as "dose tobacco-sign people." Of another trip, undertaken in order to describe the hunting of big game, I remember with most pleasure the manner in which my fare was changed after I had eaten fried bacon until, as Mr. Remington, who was with me, once expressed it, "it will be found sticking to our ribs when the last trump is blown." Mornings, noons, and nights we soiled the very forest with the eternal frying of pork, while we waited for the crust of snow to soften so that we could hunt without crashing about with the noise of wounded elephants. After nearly a week of this cloying experience, one of our half-breeds improvised a fishing-rod, attached a line and hook to it, and said, with a rare breach of semi-Indian reticence, "Be a good job if I catch some fish." He went an eighth of a mile in a direction in which none of us had moved, and there I, following him, found a beautiful, snow-blanketed lake stocked with a primeval abundance of trout. I laughed then, and have laughed ever since at the thought, when it occurred to me, that we might never have known there was a change of diet within one hundred miles, if we had not eaten pork till it turned the cast-iron stomach of that half-breed.

One of my journeys was through Cuba from end to end, and as I was commissioned only to describe the scenery and hotels for the edification of tourists, and was to do it in a hurry, I was disinclined to waste any time upon a study of the Spanish tongue. The first man I met who spoke English was a patriot tobacconist, who loved my country and wanted Cuba joined to it. "Write down in Spanish," said I, "a sufficient number of handy phrases to carry me through the island."

On a piece of brittle, brown, straw paper he wrote the Spanish equivalents of about twenty words and sentences, and with that in my pocket I journeyed through the island with only one mishap. As I remember them, the things he wrote down were: "How much? I want breakfast—dinner—supper; wine. I want to go to ——. Hurry up. No hurry. Yes, please. No, thank you. I do not speak Spanish. I do not understand. Can I have a room here? I want pen, ink, and paper. I am an American. How far is it to ——? All right." That prince in Scheherezade's tale did not get about much more easily or pleasantly on his magic carpet than did I with my square of wrapping paper; but on one day the unforeseen happened and I needed all the Spanish that I had not got.

I had taken a cab from Matanzas to the Yumuri Valley, and on the way—outside the city, in a deserted neighborhood—the driver stopped his horse. I got out and said "Hurry up." The driver shook his head, waved his hands, and appeared to swear terribly. I consulted my brown-paper lexicon and said "No hurry," and retreated into the cab and away from the frightful heat of the sun. The driver descended from his box and came to the cab door, in front of which he delivered an oration which, for earnestness, eloquence, and the other qualities that move men can seldom have been equalled. I said, "I do not understand." He sat down upon a rock and looked at me with mute helplessness—the picture of abandonment to despair. After a time I said again, "Hurry up." Then he arose and once more relieved himself in a torrent of burning Spanish. I shrugged my shoulders. He went on. He appealed to me, pleading with his hands outstretched. I pulled out my brown paper and consulted it. I decided to tell him that I wanted the next meal in the order of the day, though I had but just eaten. His fiery speech continued, so I said, "Hurry up," and then appeared to relent and remarked, "No hurry," adding that I was an American, that I did not speak Spanish, that I did not understand, that I wanted to go to the valley, and how far was it. I utilized nearly everything that was on my paper and that could assist me in seeming to converse with him. At last he wrung his hands, addressed himself to Heaven, mounted his box, and drove ahead. I hope he has repented of his profanity (if he was profane), so that we may meet in heaven, where there will be no Spanish. Then I shall find out what it was that he wanted to tell me.

Great stress has been laid upon the value of

the truth in the reports of a correspondent, yet there are times when the whole truth would jar upon the general tone or subject of a piece of work. One may not dwell upon the appearance of a new mode of hair-dressing in describing a funeral, or upon the high stakes that obtain in army poker when the address of a general to the West Point cadets is the subject in hand. I was reporting Virginia politics once, during an exciting campaign, and was—in the course of the work—in a characteristically beautiful part of the Blue Ridge region. Night fell, and with it rain. The Democratic candidate and a score of his friends, of whom I was one, repaired to a little railway-station which rose out of a great plaza of liquid mud, like a light-house in a harbor. The great, ten-acre sea of liquid mud was dimly streaked by the faint reflections of the yellow lights of the houses that stood around it. At first I could see little else than the mud and the lights, but presently I noticed a queer, floundering, wallowing, black object out in the heart of the open square. It was as if it might have been a grampus that had dropped from the clouds. It flopped about and rose and tumbled and rolled like a stranded fish of at least that size. I called the attention of my distinguished friend to it, and we splashed out to where it was. And there we found a little knot of men bending over and looking at the same thing, which was nothing less than a couple of citizens closely wrapped in each other's arms and fighting in the mud — one under and the other on top. The rain pelted them and the mud flew as they fought and struggled, and their feet and arms were flung about. One was a distinguished Democratic leader and the other was a pillar of the Republican party. I suggested that it was a pity that they should fight, and that some one ought to interfere and bid them behave themselves. My friend then called out his name and added that he would like to know what it was all about.

"Well, sir," said the man who was on top, resting his fists while he spoke; "my name is Hazel, of Hazel Court House, Hazel County, Virginia, sir, and I am a Democrat. This man said that he agreed with everything that the Republican candidate for Governor has said, and among other statements which that candidate has made are some which reflect upon a Virginian's honor, sir. These and all the other things, sir, this man has repeated and says he will stand by. That is why I'm a-licking him."

At that point there was a muddy convulsion, a splash, a twist—and the Republican was on top. Landing a neat and effective blow on the now silenced mouth of his antagonist, the man on top paused for breath, and then spoke:

"Sir," said he, "my name is Wisely, of Wiselyville, Wisely Township, and there never was a Wisely yet that wouldn't stand by his words, sir, if he died for it. And" (here he punctuated his remarks with a dig in the Democrat's ribs) "there never was a Wisely yet that was licked by a Hazel, so you can make up your mind I'll never take back what I say."

"Mr. Ralph," said my friend, "this is, as you see, a fair fight, and in this part of the country we never interfere in such a case. but let the best man win."

We waded back to the railway-station and from that point watched the battle, in which, once again, the antagonists took the form of a submarine monster in its dying throes.

THE END